International Facility Management

Innovation in the Built Environment

Series advisors

Carolyn Hayles, University of Bath
Richard Kirkham, University of Manchester
Andrew Knight, Nottingham Trent University
Stephen Pryke, University College London
Steve Rowlinson, University of Hong Kong
Derek Thomson, Loughborough University
Sara Wilkinson, University of Technology, Sydney

Innovation in the Built Environment (IBE) is a new book series for the construction industry published jointly by the Royal Institute of Chartered Surveyors and Wiley-Blackwell. It addresses issues of current research and practitioner relevance and takes an international perspective, drawing from research applications and case studies worldwide.

- Presents the latest thinking on the processes that influence the design, construction and management of the built environment

- Based on strong theoretical concepts and draws on both established techniques for analysing the processes that shape the built environment – and on those from other disciplines

- Embraces a comparative approach, allowing best practice to be put forward

- Demonstrates the contribution that effective management of built environment processes can make

Books in the IBE series

Akintoye & Beck: *Policy, Finance and Management for Public-Private Partnerships*
Booth, Hammond, Lamond & Proverbs: *Solutions for Climate Change Challenges in the Built Environment*
Boussabaine: *Risk Pricing Strategies for Public-Private Partnership Projects*
Kirkham: *Whole Life-Cycle Costing*
London: *Construction Internationalisation*
Lu & Sexton: *Innovation in Small Professional Practices in the Built Environment*
Pryke: *Construction Supply Chain Management: Concepts and Case Studies*
Roper & Borello: *International Facility Management*
Senaratne & Sexton: *Managing Change in Construction Projects*
Wilkinson, Remøy & Langston: *Sustainable Building Adaptation*

For full details please see http://eu.wiley.com/WileyCDA/Section/id-811341.html.

We welcome proposals for new, high-quality, research-based books which are academically rigorous and informed by the latest thinking; please contact Madeleine Metcalfe.

Madeleine Metcalfe
Senior Commissioning Editor
Wiley Blackwell
9600 Garsington Road
Oxford OX4 2DQ
mmetcalfe@wiley.com

International Facility Management

Kathy O. Roper

Associate Professor and Chair of Integrated Facility Management
Georgia Institute of Technology
U.S.A

&

Lisa J. Borello

Editor
Georgia Institute of Technology
U.S.A

WILEY Blackwell

Registered Office
John Wiley & Sons, Ltd, The Atrium, Southern Gate, Chichester, West Sussex, PO19 8SQ, United Kingdom.

Editorial Offices
9600 Garsington Road, Oxford, OX4 2DQ, United Kingdom.
The Atrium, Southern Gate, Chichester, West Sussex, PO19 8SQ, United Kingdom.

For details of our global editorial offices, for customer services and for information about how to apply for permission to reuse the copyright material in this book please see our website at www.wiley.com/wiley-blackwell.

Library of Congress Cataloging-in-Publication Data

International facility management / [compiled by] Kathy O. Roper and Lisa J. Borello.
  pages   cm.
 Includes bibliographical references and index.
 ISBN 978-0-470-67400-0 (cloth)
1. Facility management. I. Roper, Kathy O. II. Borello, Lisa J., 1977–
 TS155.I57777 2014
 658.2–dc23
                                      2013024197

A catalogue record for this book is available from the British Library.

Wiley also publishes its books in a variety of electronic formats. Some content that appears in print may not be available in electronic books.

Cover image: Meaden Creative
Cover design by ©iStockphoto/Matejay

Set in 10.5/12.5pt Sabon by SPi Publisher Services, Pondicherry, India
Printed and bound in Malaysia by Vivar Printing Sdn Bhd

1   2014

Contents

About the Authors

Robert L. Barnes is Director, Facility Operations & Real Estate at Novartis Institutes for BioMedical Research in Cambridge, Massachusetts. He is a Certified Facility Manager and Master of Corporate Real Estate with more than 25 years of experience, including his U.S. Navy career.

Lisa J. Borello has more than 13 years of experience in writing and editing scholarly and non-scholarly work. Dr. Borello completed her doctorate degree in Sociology of Science & Technology at Georgia Institute of Technology.

Manish Dixit is a PhD Candidate in the Department of Construction Science at Texas A&M University. He is a Leadership in Energy and Environmental Design Accredited Professional (LEED AP) and a registered architect and landscape architect in India, and he has published research articles in peer-reviewed facility management journals.

Robert R. Friedmann is Professor Emeritus of Criminal Justice at Georgia State University's Andrew Young School of Policy Studies and the Founding Director of the Georgia International Law Enforcement Exchange (GILEE). Dr. Friedmann is the author of seven books on criminal justice, policing, security and terrorism as well as numerous articles and research reports. He served on numerous public safety and blue ribbon commissions, advised law enforcement agencies and provided training to law enforcement and corporate security leaders.

Robert (Bob) W. Hayes is Managing Director of the Security Executive Council, a research and advisory services firm that specializes in risk mitigation. Hayes has more than 25 years of experience in developing security programs and providing security services.

Chris Hodges is a founding Principal of Facility Engineering Associates with 30 years of experience in engineering and facility management (FM). He is an adjunct faculty member in George Mason University's certificate program in Facility Management. He has authored and presented for the International Facility Management Association (IFMA), the Association of Higher Education Facilities Officers (APPA) and the American Society of Interior Designers (ASID), and at several Middle Eastern, European and Asian FM conferences.

Sarel Lavy is Associate Professor and Graduate Program Coordinator – Construction Science and Associate Director, CRS Center at Texas A&M University. He is also the new Co-editor of *Facilities* and a frequent contributor to FM academic journals.

Kathy O. Roper is Associate Professor and Chair of Integrated Facility Management at Georgia Institute of Technology, where she teaches graduate courses in FM, project management and corporate real estate. Following a 23-year career in corporate, government and not for profit facility and real estate management, she is also Co-founder and Co-editor of the open-access *International Facility Management Journal*.

Matthew P. Tucker is a Senior Lecturer in Facilities Management at Liverpool John Moores University. Matthew's background is in service improvement and he specializes in strategic FM research, with a particular focus on customer satisfaction, environmental sustainability, organizational behaviour and workplace productivity.

Abbreviations

AECFM	architecture, engineering, construction and facility management
ANSI	American National Standards Institute
APPA	Leadership in Educational Facilities (formerly known as the Association of Physical Plant Administrators)
ASHRAE	American Society of Heating, Refrigerating and Air-Conditioning Engineers
BAS	building automation system
BCP	business continuity program
BEPS	building energy performance simulation
BIA	business impact analysis
BIFM	British Institute of Facilities Management
BIM	building information modeling
BOMA	Building Owners and Managers Association
BREEAM	British Research Environment Environmental Assessment Methodology
BTU	British thermal unit
CAFM	computer-aided facility management
CCET	competencies, credentials, education and training
CDP	Carbon Disclosure Project
CEO	Chief Executive Officer
CFO	Chief Finance Officer
CMM	capabilities maturity model
CMMS	computerized maintenance management system
COO	Chief Operating Officer
CoreNet	Corporate Real Estate Network Global
CPMS	customer performance measurement system
CRE	corporate real estate
CRM	client relationship management
CSA	Canadian Standards Association
CSR	corporate social responsibility
DMA	disclosure on management approach
EI	environmental indicator (referenced in Global Reporting Initiative documentation)

EN	European Standard (approved by one of the European Standardization Organizations – ESOs)
EOC	emergency operations centre
EU	European Union
EUI	energy utilization index
FCI	facility condition index
FM	facility (or facilities) management
FMA	Facility Management Association Australia
GDP	gross domestic product
GRI	Global Reporting Initiative
HVAC	heating, ventilation and air conditioning
ICT	information and communications technology
IFC	industry foundation class
IFMA	International Facility Management Association
IPD	integrated project delivery
ISO	International Standards Organization
IT	information technology
IWMS	integrated workplace management system
kBTU	thousand British thermal units (unit of measure)
KPI	key performance indicator
LCCA	life-cycle cost analysis
LEED	Leadership in Energy and Environmental Design
MAC	move, add and change (usually an activity)
MJ	megajoule
MOU	memorandum (or memoranda) of understanding
NFPA	National Fire Protection Association (US)
O&M	operations and maintenance
PFI	private finance initiative
POE	post-occupancy evaluation
PPP	public-private partnership
RFP	request for proposal(s)
SLA	service-level agreement
SME	subject matter expert
USDOE	US Department of Energy
USEPA	US Environmental Protection Agency
USGBC	US Green Building Council
VOC	volatile organic compound
WOW	ways of working

Introduction

In titling this edition, we editors, who have close ties to the International Facility Management Association, the largest association of facility professionals world-wide, chose to use the term *International Facility Management*. In business, confusing terminology in the field – such as international, multinational, transnational and global – often leads to misunderstandings, so we want to clearly state that we are advocating for a world viewpoint on the nature and dimensions of facility management. The general definition of things or organizations that are described as 'global' refers to the entire world, without regard to country or geographical location. The word 'international' frequently refers to organizations or things that involve a relationship between two or more nations. Since organizations may exist in one or many nations, we chose this wording to correspond to the relationship of managing the built environment across the world, whether in one or many locations.

Because relationships are a key element of facility management, this relationship focus is one that we hope to bring to the forefront. Great practices and research related to facility management are being performed in many nations, but rather than concealing these efforts, we hope to promote multinational sharing. Hence, our authors come from many parts of the world and range from consultants to academics and practitioners. As a still emerging profession with a short 35-year history, we continue to call upon related professions for expertise. As FM moves from technical to more strategic dimensions, as the value becomes better understood and recognized and as state-of-the-art concepts are shared around the globe, the facility management practitioners, supporters, suppliers and senior business leaders all benefit from this growth.

The worldwide impact of technological advances, changing demographics, required attention to sustainability and security as well as general shifts in business all require that facility management continues to rapidly advance to keep pace. Aging infrastructure in developed countries, new opportunities in emerging economies and worldwide economic developments all demand that facility management adapts and changes. We see a new wave of dramatic change underway and believe that facility management is changing just as dramatically. The focus and impetus for this book is that change. We hope to capture some of the highlights, updates and anticipated needs to enlighten the reader to action; to remain alert for ongoing change; and to rapidly educate and develop the next generation of new facility management professionals.

Facility Management: Changing Global Viewpoints and Maturity

Kathy O. Roper and Lisa J. Borello

Georgia Institute of Technology, Atlanta, GA

While aspects of the profession have been practiced for decades, facility management is considered a relatively new profession. From its origins with the term *facility management* (FM) in the late 1970s, the two primary drivers of its creation were the acceptance of open-office concepts across Europe and the United States and the integration of computing technology into the general workforce. These two drivers essentially changed the landscape of workplaces, opening designs and providing a new focus for management as they moved out of hard-walled offices to oversee their employees, and as employees and managers began to transmit information electronically. Volumes have been written on each of these phenomena, but dramatic shifts are underway again today that rival the changes within workplaces; these shifts are changing the nature and the value of the FM profession, causing FM to become more strategic, more valued, and a critical component of businesses today.

As workplace design changed in the 1970s and 1980s to accommodate computing technologies and reveal less enclosed working areas, the developed nations of Europe and North America began to study the impacts and effects that these new workplaces provided. Early research in the United Kingdom helped to set the first FM research agenda focused on learning, as well as educating individuals in the new art and science of FM. Around the same time, US researchers began to see value in understanding how the environment impacts workers and their productivity. This "holy grail" of understanding and calculating productivity remains at the forefront of research today. In the ensuing 30-plus years, more has been learned and gradual shifts in the business

International Facility Management, First Edition. Kathy O. Roper and Lisa J. Borello.
© 2014 John Wiley & Sons, Ltd. Published 2014 by John Wiley & Sons, Ltd.

environment are accommodating the elevation of FM "from the boiler room to the board room."

Today, we see new drivers of change in workplaces and workplace management. Facility professionals across the world are now being asked, "What is our carbon footprint?" "How can we meet new guidelines and regulations around sustainability?" "Have we ensured that our facilities are secure and prepared for emergencies and disasters?" And "How can we use our workplace to attract and retain the best employees?" These and other questions now drive the FM function to be more strategic and more involved in business decision making, and elevate the FM professional to a new level of expert who is prepared to help guide the organization environmentally, socially, and, of course, financially.

Primarily driven by the sustainability movement across the world, facility professionals not only deal with the design, construction, and operation of facilities but also now provide these functions with an eye toward improving triple-bottom-line accounting. Because FM is the second largest expense behind employee salaries, and is an influence on the productivity of those salaried employees, FM professionals are indeed valuable contributors to any organization's senior management team.

As organizations become more integrated in world markets, the number of multinational organizations is expanding. From 1991 to 2001, headcounts within multinationals surged from 24 to 54 million, and their turnover doubled (Delmas-Marty, 2008). Even organizations operating in only one country now often utilize outsourced labor, or procure materials from various international locations, so global awareness has become a new competency of the facility professional. In addition to global expansion, the breadth of knowledge required to effectively manage facilities has become tremendous. As technology, sustainability, and demographics lurch forward, facility professionals add responsibilities to an already broad array of demands.

Overview of the Volume

This chapter provides a broad overview of the dramatic change currently underway in business and its impacts on FM. As businesses grow and expand, facility professionals grow and expand their roles. This volume explores a range of issues of growing importance to the field of FM now and in the future.

Authored by Robert Barnes, Chapter 2 provides a complete view of the skills, education, and knowledge required for effective FM today. Barnes offers an overview of many resources for facility professionals and provides a framework to consider if one is attempting to advance within the profession. He also provides a summary of the various organizations that support FM broadly or by industry. Certifications are also described as a means of demonstrating competency at varying levels of

FM. As Barnes suggests, as the nature of the field changes and as modern buildings become even more sophisticated, the need for new skills and formal training of FM professionals is critical.

In Chapter 3, Kathy Roper provides an update to information on service provider relationships. Originally published in 2011 in *Managing the Professional Practice in the Built Environment*, this chapter includes an update to focus global information on the provision side of FM. Originally titled "How Thin to Win?" the chapter and its updates provide a clear view of the need for both the hiring organization and service provider to work amicably to support one another in order to provide a win–win relationship.

Globalization is the topic for Chapter 4 and provides an overview of major differences in perspective in various regions of the world, as well as updates on research foci from each of the regions. Author Kathy Roper explores trends and FM needs, as well as the education and training out-look, in Africa, Asia, Australasia, South America, the Middle East, Europe, and North America. While local demands and priorities exist, the desire to advance FM worldwide is promoted with suggestions on learning across regions. Even industrialized nations can learn from some of the newer tricks being used within the industrializing nations. The ability to share information and learning will benefit the profession worldwide.

Chapter 5, titled "Sustainability and Carbon Reporting," evaluates the role of the facility manager in sustainability and carbon reporting. While the facility manager is typically not in the role of making organizational decisions related to overall operations, author Chris Hodges argues that in the area of sustainability, the FM professional can play an important consulting role by persuasively demonstrating the value of sustainability efforts and the impact they provide to the overall organization. A thorough review of how facilities impact carbon emissions and a global reporting methodology are covered here, as well as more general principles of sustainability and sustainability guidelines.

Preparing for emergencies – both natural and man-made – is critical for ensuring that businesses and operations run smoothly. In Chapter 6, authors Robert Friedmann and Bob Hayes outline the core framework for developing a business continuity program (BCP), and they outline BCP planning principles that can be adapted to a variety of organizations and can be utilized by facility managers in executing comprehensive business continuity and emergency response plans. As developers of the Security Executive Council, the authors have provided direct resources that corporations and other large organizations can use to develop their emergency preparedness and business continuity planning.

As workplaces and the very concept of "the workplace" have changed, facility managers have new challenges and opportunities. In Chapter 7, Kathy Roper explores the dramatic changes to Knowledge Age work, the rise of distributed work, new management challenges, and the impacts to FM, offering suggestions on how facility managers can play a role in changing the workplace itself, provide motivation for increased productivity of workers, and benefit the bottom line of the organization.

In Chapter 8, Matthew Tucker explores performance measurement, benchmarking, and their applications to the FM field, and he provides information on tools such as the balanced scorecard and key performance indicators for consideration and use. He argues that FM performance measurement needs to go beyond just quantitative indicators, such as the physical infrastructure and numerical measures, to qualitative measures that focus on the organization and on improving the quality of service delivery. By understanding the importance of measuring people, processes, and place within an organization and their integration with the core business function, he argues that the efficiency of measuring the quality of FM services will improve.

Sarel Lavy and Manish Dixit provide an in-depth look at four major industries in Chapter 9, exploring the needs and demographics of each. Examining education facilities, public sector buildings, healthcare facilities, and office buildings, Lavy and Dixit outline some of the common themes found among these four major types of facilities, as well as significant differences, with implications for the FM professional.

The book concludes with Chapter 10, which provides an outlook to the future. While we have not found the FM crystal ball, we have found a number of indicators of important issues that will influence the field over the next decade. Beyond that time horizon, we shudder to imagine the scenarios, be they *Mad Max: Beyond Thunderdome* and *Fury Road*, or more akin to *2010: A Space Odyssey* (updated to 2050, of course!).

References

Delmas-Marty, M, (2008). GoodPlanet.info: environmental news and related issues. Available at: http://www.goodplanet.info/eng/Contenu/Points-de-vues/Globalisation-et-societes-transnationales (accessed 22 October 2012).

Roper, K.O. (2011). How thin to win? In *Managing the professional practice in the built environment*, ed. H. Smyth. Oxford: Wiley-Blackwell, pp. 161–172.

Competencies, Credentials, Education, and Training

Robert L. Barnes

Novartis Institutes of BioMedical Research, Cambridge, MA

As a comparatively new management discipline, facility management (FM) has made great progress in developing as a profession, especially since 1981 when a professional association was organized, the International Facility Management Association (IFMA). Of course, the function itself has existed since antiquity, when buildings were primarily shelters before evolving into places of controlled environments to enhance comfort and productivity. Yet, those who maintained buildings in the industrial era, before formal FM and IFMA, were typically tradesmen, technicians, or plant engineers focused more on building system reliance with no regard for workplace strategy and services. There was little if any collaboration with others with similar responsibilities in the industry on best practices, and consequently FM was viewed as more of a utility plant operation; necessary, but out of sight, out of mind. Aside from tradesmen, few managers and leaders considered FM as having a professional career path. Engineers assigned to FM often viewed it as a detour from the norm, or they managed the facility along with other engineering responsibilities.

With the increasing sophistication and complexity of modern building structures and systems, the need became apparent for facilities, or the built environment, to be managed by staff with a versatile and cohesive set of competencies, including alignment with the objectives of the business enterprise. So as the knowledge workplace grew in importance over the past few decades, it became necessary to complement FM technical expertise with leadership and business competencies.

International Facility Management, First Edition. Kathy O. Roper and Lisa J. Borello.
© 2014 John Wiley & Sons, Ltd. Published 2014 by John Wiley & Sons, Ltd.

As FM practitioners with leadership and business acumen became more prevalent, a career track "from the boiler room to the boardroom," or at least to higher echelons of organizations, began to take shape. Since the inception of IFMA, the competency areas have been refined continually along with a viable FM career framework. In the more successful situations, FM executives even occupy a seat in the boardroom or at least have regular access to the C-suite, although such access is still relatively uncommon in most organizations. Also, renewed focus in the technician level of FM has occurred with the need for better understanding of the building life cycle and interdependencies of systems, including new green technologies.

With clear career pathways at all levels of the FM profession, and many specialty forms of professional associations spawning since IFMA was established over 30 years ago, this is a good point to question whether FM exhibits the marks of a professional discipline. In conducting a similar assessment of the corporate real estate (CRE) profession, Dohner (2004) cited these requirements:

- A universally recognized practice, service, or management discipline
- Graduate-level education, a certified basic level of competence, and a minimum level of practical experience with a requirement for continuous learning
- A formalized process to encourage, recognize, and disseminate research in the discipline
- Professional associations and publications to convene the industry to exchange ideas, innovations, and best practices
- A self-governing body responsible for setting and maintaining industry metrics, standards, and practices
- Some formalized process to provide for those in need (i.e. without adequate resources) to obtain the required services of the discipline
- A self-governing body to set and maintain standards of competency, with the authority and responsibility to discipline those members who are incompetent, unethical, or otherwise unfit to practice.

Another integral mark of a profession is that it must have a credible and robust career framework. With the exception of the last item in Dohner's list (which is not germane to the topic of this chapter), FM has attained each mark, yet not quite to the depth of other well-established professions, particularly in regard to the level of graduate-level education available, and, more importantly, the level to which members aspiring to become opinion leaders with impact beyond the FM profession itself take advantage of these opportunities. More on this will be provided in this chapter.

One of the most important aspects of a profession's authenticity is how it is recognized by other disciplines, especially in respect to the enterprise itself. Waheed and Fernie (2009) noted the gap between the aspiration of strategic relevance and reality in addressing the question of whether FM is a legitimate discipline with associated theories, research, and practice. For some organizations, FM is in the rut of being viewed as a support organization rather than one that can lead enterprise workplace strategy and ensure equilibrium in facility operations and services. This view is perpetuated when C-suite executives consign facilities to the operational realm and overlook the opportunity to grant FM strategic relevance.

As depicted in Table 2.1, traditional perceptions of the profession must yield to a new way of thinking. With that under consideration, who can best influence shifting the paradigm to encompass such relevance for the profession? The answer is the practitioners within the FM profession; otherwise, the status quo will ensue because recipients of FM services tend to focus on short-sighted needs.

CCET Framework as the Linchpin to Transformation

The linchpin to elevating the profile of the profession is an adaptable and robust framework of competencies, credentials, education, and training (CCET) for filling and nurturing the pipeline of FM talent that is needed to fuel the business environment. The CCET framework is the catalyst for transforming FM knowledge into core competence that is of value to the enterprise.

Table 2.1   Facility management (FM) roles and perceptions (Waheed and Fernie, 2009)

Roles	Traditional perception	Proposed perception
Physical assets and services	Exploited for the effectiveness of core competences	A core competence itself
FM	Support function	Strategic input permeating all functions
FM knowledge	Borrowed; reliant on other disciplines	Discipline-specific knowledge, based on its execution and environmental constraints
Formal bodies	Networking	Regulation, education of clients, and awareness

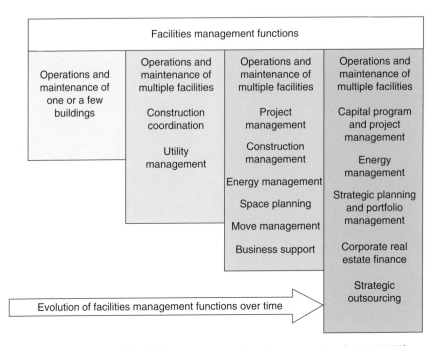

Figure 2.1   Evolution of facilities management functions over time (APPA, 2002).

As depicted in Figure 2.1, FM knowledge has progressed along with its functions, mostly in a linear track corresponding to the evolution of outsourcing. To attain universal recognition as a professional discipline, FM practitioners must sharply increase the linear progression to include the strategic elements in the right-hand column of Figure 2.1.

To enable the FM profession to shift to strategic relevance within the enterprise, the CCET framework needs to be renovated to fuel and sustain the talent pipeline. Let us first examine the basic dependencies and the status quo. As with most professions, FM consists of managerial and technical ladders, and career stages of entry, mid-, and advanced levels within each. What is unconventional about the FM profession is that the managerial and executive ranks were nearly entirely filled by midcareer crossovers, many of who were on the cusp of retirement. The CCET framework was therefore geared to accommodating these individuals, who preferred trade association networking, conference seminars, and credential-related training over education provided by accredited academic institutions. As a result, the influx of talent from the millennial generation cannot keep pace with the attrition because of the paucity of programs to attract early interest by high school graduates matriculating into college. When the relatively brief window of opportunity closes, then the FM profession draws from a niche of students affiliated with the limited FM undergraduate academic programs, or has to count on those who later discover the profession through graduate

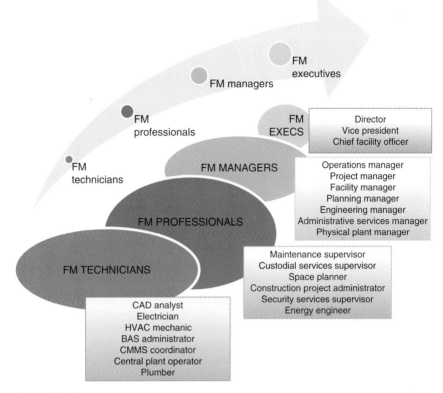

Figure 2.2   "Tech-to-exec" career model.

school (which has likewise limited availability) or isolated crossover opportunities once employed.

A general career pathway with common positions is shown in Figure 2.2. The CCET framework must be dynamic and pace the model to sustain the flourishing global built environment. And the framework must be bilateral, providing both bandwidth and depth in mastering complexity and asserting strategic leadership.

Authoritative and Influential Stakeholders

There is an extensive network of stakeholders of various degrees of influence within and on the periphery of the FM profession who are contributing to the body of knowledge (BOK) from which requisite competencies are derived. The competencies in turn guide the development of the CCET framework, looping back to the leading institutional stakeholders (i.e. professional associations and accredited academic institutions), which we will now examine in terms of their respective roles and contributions.

FM and CRE Professional Associations

Referring to IFMA's framework as a comparative baseline, this section is an overview of how each association develops its architecture for competencies, including advanced research for propagating knowledge to its membership through training, credentialing, conference programs, and networking. IFMA, APPA, CoreNet, and the Building Owners and Managers Association (BOMA) International are the major FM and CRE trade associations based in the United States.

The International Facility Management Association (IFMA)

The backbone of IFMA is the vitality of its membership, which participates in its network of chapters, councils, and communities of practice throughout the world. The chapters provide local networking for peers, mentoring, sharing of best practices, learning programs, specific resources (including job referral services), and leadership opportunities. IFMA-sanctioned chapters are autonomous communities, and each offers a range of functions and services that can accelerate the career of the FM professional who actively participates. Similarly, FM professionals often consider supplementing chapter participation by joining councils or communities of practice in order to affiliate with peers who share even more specific interests. Some of the councils have established online communities in which members probe others for best practices, solicit expert advice, and engage in narrative streams of consciousness on topics that spawn a variety of blog-style viewpoints.

IFMA's professional development and certification program for the FM practitioner is defined by eleven intertwined competency areas that form the basis for attaining its entry-level, knowledge-based credential, Facility Management Professional (FMP). The next level is the industry standard credential, Certified Facility Manager (CFM), which is awarded based on work experience, knowledge, and a comprehensive examination. Furthermore, to maintain the CFM credential, one must meet a high certifying standard for continuing education and experience. Design of the multifaceted IFMA training program, from online delivery to instructor-led courses, is based on the competency areas for the FM professional who prepares to attain this top career credential. Recognizing the contemporary significance of a facility's impact on the environment and community, IFMA created a specialty credential, the Sustainability Facility Professional (SFP). IFMA also has an exclusive Fellows Program intended for those who have made exceptional contributions to the profession, a capstone achievement requiring nomination by a colleague and a jury decision on whether to grant the designation.

Throughout each year, IFMA coordinates symposia and conferences, including the most respected annual tradeshow in the industry, the World

Workplace Conference & Expo, and the annual Facility Fusion Conference & Expo, which provides a fusion of FM-centric education, best practices, solutions, and leadership training. In addition to the extensive educational programs and networking available at these conferences, there are opportunities to speak, moderate, and instruct by those who want to set themselves apart from their peers. IFMA also maintains the Facility Management Knowledge Center, an online repository of 24/7 on-demand recordings, webinars, webcasts, white papers, and online courses all geared to providing continuing education units and credential maintenance points.

A vital aspect of the IFMA CCET framework is its research program, which is focused on industry surveys that form the basis for benchmark reports and forecast trend reports, public policy reports, strategy guides, and in-depth research studies of current topics. To facilitate real-time building comparative analysis, IFMA established the Benchmarks Exchange (BEX), a secure online survey management system. IFMA also produces and advocates a wide range of publications, from its own *Facility Management Journal* to professional books and reports. Not only do these offer opportunities for advanced learning, but also those who seek a position of thought leadership can write articles for publication in *FM Journal* or the *International Journal of Facility Management*, referred to in this chapter.

To advance FM as a profession, IFMA established in 1990 a separate entity, the IFMA Foundation, as a nonprofit 501(c)(3) corporation. The IFMA Foundation works for the public good with a vision to "expand the knowledge of the built environment in a changing world through scholarships, education and research." Its focus undergirds the CCET framework, including the following:

- Scholarships for those preparing to enter the field of FM
- An accredited degree program designed to recognize and encourage the strengthening of current, valid FM education degrees and to assist in the development of new FM degree programs
- Funding research projects that strengthen the multifaceted knowledge and skills of FM professionals. Its research advocacy includes the *International Journal of Facility Management*, a peer-reviewed professional journal.
- Maintaining FMpedia, a dynamic, real-time, Internet-based glossary open to any contributors within the FM profession.

Evidence of global recognition of the IFMA CCET framework is that many of its training and credential programs have been exported to other FM professional associations globally. These associations, along with others, have CCET frameworks with some elements common to those of IFMA. We will note among the following associations what elements are distinct and worth consideration as best practices.

APPA

APPA, based in Alexandria, Virginia, is an FM trade association focused on maintaining educational facilities in the United States, including partners in several other countries. Its original name, Association of Physical Plant Administrators of Universities, is obsolete, yet the APPA acronym remains as its brand identity. APPA has a strong central support staff, and its proximity to Washington, D.C., is not coincidental in terms of its advocacy role. Similar to the other national FM associations, APPA has a network of local chapters for its membership, although because of its smaller membership base (about 4800 members compared to 23,000 in IFMA and 17,000 in BOMA), its focus is on supporting member-led regional organizations.

APPA has developed an extensive Body of Knowledge (BOK), which it refers to as the "collected wisdom, experience, processes, and facts that both inform a profession and provide the solid foundation from which continuous improvements and innovative change can occur." It builds upon and updates the contents of APPA's major reference book, *Facilities Management: A Manual for Plant Administration*, which focuses on its four core competencies. APPA keeps the BOK current through an active editorial board that ensures peer review of content through the Center for Facilities Research (CFaR), supported by peer review panels, and has a strong external focus (including government, regulatory agencies, etc.). Review of the BOK is accessible through a searchable digital database.

In 2005, APPA determined the need to establish a credentialing and certification program, so it formed a task force that recommended a two-tier system, using the BOK as the foundation for two credentials: Educational Facilities Professional (EFP) and Certified Educational Facilities Professional (CEFP). The APPA system is analogous to IFMA's two-tier FMP and CFM credential program. Both programs focus on mastery of expertise in core competencies, commitment to growth, and leadership.

APPA has a Fellows Program intended for thought leaders, who can apply for the Fellow designation. The APPA Fellow application prescribes specific and challenging requirements, including a research project, education, publication of an article, and professional endorsements. Its thought leadership opportunities include the following:

- Thought Leader Series of summits on current topics and trends
- APPA publishes a bimonthly professional magazine, *Facilities Manager*, and encourages its members to contribute articles
- The Center for Facilities Research, in which members are encouraged to propose or undertake facilities-related research projects with the goal of advancing the BOK
- Advisory opportunities within the Facility Performance Indicator (FPI) training and consulting services offered to member sites

▪ Qualified peer evaluators who conduct institutional assessments through the Facilities Management Evaluation Program (FMEP).

CoreNet Global

The Corporate Real Estate Network (CoreNet) convenes the CRE end user and occupier on the demand side with the supply side of the CRE value chain, including the diversity of service providers and economic developers. As the workplace has grown in significance, CoreNet has evolved beyond conventional commercial real estate issues to encompass the broader context of real estate (i.e. integrating the management of corporate assets, the workplace, and infrastructure). Many, if not most, enterprises have consolidated FM and real estate within the same reporting structure. There remain distinct differences in the technical skill sets between FM and real estate professionals, and senior leaders are often responsible for both functions, with a common interest in developing and managing the workplace infrastructure, albeit from somewhat different perspectives.

CoreNet Global supports a global network of chapters that provide learning, collaboration, and career development opportunities; other associations do the same, but the aspect that sets apart CoreNet chapters is CoreNet's chapter-to-chapter exchange (C2CX). Recognizing that education is critical to the future success and growth of CoreNet and its members, CoreNet determined that chapter learning programs need to expand to support global participation of chapters at every stage of development and to strengthen the learning experience at the chapter level for its members. C2CX is a web-enabled globally accessible platform that provides a central repository of vetted speaker talent and programs to enable resource sharing in a financially sustainable way.

CoreNet offers a professional credential, Master of Corporate Real Estate (MCR), which designates special competence and experience as a CRE executive. This credential emphasizes aspects of the core business (e.g. case study methodology, workplace strategy, the impact of global markets, and enterprise alignment), whereas the FM credentials noted here focus on the knowledge and abilities used in the practice of FM. CoreNet also provides a second tier to its credential program, the Senior Leader Corporate Real Estate (SLCR) credential, which is specifically structured for the thought leader. The SLCR provides a series of forums on change leadership, enterprise program management, financial leadership, and others, including one on positioning and designing the optimal CRE organization. This thought leadership structure is precisely geared to elevating the profile of CRE by crafting it as the "business of the business."

The searchable online Knowledge Center provides to members free of charge an extensive repository of publications, articles, white papers, research reports, surveys, case studies, press releases, presentations, and periodicals covering many topics. CoreNet publishes a bimonthly magazine on CRE and workplace issues, *The Leader*, and encourages contributions from members and profiles its senior leaders.

To tap into the distributed intelligence of the CRE community as a whole, CoreNet sets up communities of practice for ongoing collaboration among its members to share critical knowledge and discover solutions to common problems. Current practice areas include the workplace, strategic and portfolio planning, and sustainability. Recognizing the vital importance of component leadership (i.e. volunteer member leaders of chapters, communities of practice, and special interest groups), CoreNet devised a website dedicated to the development of best practices and strong leaders who are committed to working together to innovate CoreNet as the preeminent knowledge source for the industry. CoreNet also operates a social media website, NetWORK, complete with online community, blogs, and other features.

With its global emphasis, CoreNet conducts five summit conferences each year, two in North America and one each in Asia, Australia or New Zealand, and EMEA (Europe, the Middle East, and Africa). In addition to extensive learning sessions, the summits offer opportunities for members to speak and participate in special interest groups.

In the upper echelon of its CCET framework, CoreNet places a strong emphasis on developing industry opinion leaders, including the Discovery Forum, which is facilitated case-based discussions that explore the major challenges facing corporations, and how CRE executives and service providers are responding to these challenges. The series culminates in an annual Industry Leaders Roundtable during which corporate and strategic partners convene to examine trends and forces impacting CRE management, including the nature of work, the workplace, and the delivery of real estate–related services. These opinions lead to the findings published in the annual state of the industry report.

Building Owners and Managers Association International (BOMA)

The mission of BOMA International is to enhance the human, intellectual, and physical assets of the CRE industry through advocacy, education, research, standards, and information. In some ways, BOMA's constituency is a composite of the FM and CRE professions, with membership represented by building owners, managers, developers, leasing professionals, medical office building managers, corporate facility managers, asset managers, and the providers of the products and services needed to operate commercial properties.

Although the major FM and CRE trade associations all play an advocacy role toward government, BOMA points to legislative affairs as a dominant role. BOMA has full-time staff assigned to monitor and lobby pertinent legislative and regulatory issues, including building codes and standards, utilities, tax relief, telecommunications, the environment, private property rights, risk assessment, insurance, and other topics. Its website has a Legislative Action Center that prompts members to action on state and federal legislation that is germane to the commercial real estate industry. These elements form, in BOMA's CCET framework, a unique niche within the profession.

BOMA formed a separate 501(c)(3) training institute, the Building Owners and Managers Institute (BOMI), which offers industry-standard designations and professional education, which are the major components of career development. Equally important is the networking that BOMA offers in its local associations and trade shows. Members consider BOMA as the primary source of information on office building development, leasing, building operating costs, energy consumption patterns, local and national building codes, legislation, occupancy statistics, and technological developments.

BOMI coordinates the professional designation programs for BOMA, the Facilities Management Administrator (FMA) and Real Property Administrator (RPA), which underscore the BOMA focus on property management. Also, BOMI offers a unique pair of property maintenance certifications, the Systems Maintenance Technician (SMT) and Systems Maintenance Administrator (SMA). These designations and associated training programs form the foundation of a property manager CCET framework, which is sustained through networking and leadership opportunities in chapter affiliations and in participation in conferences such as the major annual BOMA conference and tradeshow.

BOMA publishes its own *The BOMA Magazine* and a series of how-to guidebooks, standards, and research reports, all available through its extensive store. Members are encouraged to participate in research studies and submit written articles to the magazine.

To encourage thought leadership among its executive members, BOMA has established regional and national advisory councils. The Regional Owners Council (ROC) assembles owner and equity partners of single- and regional-market commercial real estate firms to share experiences, discuss strategies, and compare best practices. The National Advisory Council (NAC) is an exclusive network of senior commercial real estate professionals focused on discussing the most pressing issues impacting companies with large regional, national, and international portfolios, while acting as a leadership sounding board for BOMA International.

Specialty FM and CRE Professional Associations

Apart from the major FM and CRE trade associations, there are related professional associations that specialize in niche segments of FM and CRE. This section highlights those with CCET frameworks for their members.

American Hospital Association (AHA) and American Society of Healthcare Engineers (ASHE)

The American Hospital Association (AHA) represents about 5000 hospitals, healthcare systems, networks, and providers of care. The AHA plays a dominant role in advocacy for its members in both the legislative and regulatory arenas. It also is a source of information on healthcare issues and trends, and it provides education for healthcare leaders, including a Certification Center that designs and administers certification programs to recognize mastery of well-defined bodies of knowledge within healthcare management disciplines.

For healthcare FM professionals, the AHA organized an affiliate, the American Society of Healthcare Engineers (ASHE), which offers two credentials through the Certification Center: the Certified Healthcare Facility Manager (CHFM) and Certified Healthcare Constructor (CHC). Both credentials have corresponding handbooks that detail the competencies required for attaining each. ASHE also offers a number of specialty certificates in construction and project management. ASHE is cooperating with Georgia Tech as an FM healthcare educator to develop specialized courses and is exploring a healthcare concentration within the Building Construction master's degree program.

Institute of Real Estate Management (IREM)

The Institute of Real Estate Management (IREM) supports the profession of real estate managers who manage properties. IREM offers several credentials, one of which has some similarities to BOMA's RPA designation, the Certified Property Manager (CPM).

Industrial Asset Management Council (IAMC)

Founded in 2002, the Industrial Asset Management Council (IAMC) is an association of industrial asset management and CRE executives, their suppliers and service providers, and economic developers. IAMC offers its members professional forums, leadership seminars, research roundtables, and a leadership development program that culminates in a designation as Fellow through completion of training and association service requirements. IAMC also publishes *Site Selection*, a monthly magazine focused on CRE strategy and area economic development.

Professional Retail Store Maintenance Association (PRSMA)

The Professional Retail Store Maintenance Association (PRSMA) is composed primarily of retail facility managers of multisite facilities. PRSMA considers retail FM as a specialty that requires "a retail-specific solution in the generic world of professional certification," so it devised the Retail Facility Maintenance Professional (RFMP) certification, which focuses on the unique aspects of maintaining public facilities – like disaster management and specialized equipment. PRSMA publishes a bimonthly magazine and periodic e-newsletters, coordinates a best practices white paper program, and manages an online community.

International Association of Assembly Managers (IAAM)

The International Association of Assembly Managers (IAAM) is committed to the operation of amphitheaters, arenas, auditoriums, convention centers, exhibit halls, performing arts venues, racetracks, stadiums, and university complexes. IAAM believes that managing venues that accommodate large public audiences poses unique and significant challenges in the areas of public safety, emergency preparedness, security, ancillary use as shelter, HVAC (heating, ventilation, and air conditioning) comfort control and energy management for large structures, crowd management, and other issues, hence the need for this specialty association and its own training and certification structure. For sharing of best practices and research, it has a Center for Venue Management Studies, Venue Research Institute, and Academy for Venue Safety and Security. It also has its own credential, Certified Facilities Executive (CFE), which requires a comprehensive application to sit for a competency-based exam and oral interview.

Other Global Professional Associations

There are exemplary FM CCET frameworks outside the United States, notably in Europe, Australia, and Asia (i.e. Hong Kong and Singapore), as well as emerging evidence in other countries such as Brazil. In the United Kingdom in particular, there is a diverse network among business, trade associations, government agencies, academia, and worker guilds, with a strong talent pipeline, a career track, and high societal regard for FM as a profession. This section highlights the major international FM professional associations.

British Institute of Facilities Management (BIFM)

Founded in 1993, the British Institute of Facilities Management (BIFM) is composed of over 12,000 members. BIFM's mission is part of its brand tagline, "advancing our profession" of FM. In 2008, BIFM became recognized as an awarding organization subject to the oversight of the Office of Qualifications and Examinations Regulation (Ofqual), which regulates vocational qualifications in the United Kingdom. Consequently, BIFM has an accredited Qualifications and Credit Framework (QCF) that is subject to monitoring and audit by Ofqual. The framework encompasses the entry level beginning as early as the teenage years through eight levels of professional achievement up to and including the doctorate level. There are three levels of qualification: award, certificate, and diploma. Underlying the framework is an array of documentation, including a learner's handbook and qualification charts that depict the coursework, work-based learning, assessment methods, and credit values for each achievement; these are all detailed in BIFM's special training website, www.bifm-training.com. BIFM developed an FM qual-ifications matrix, showing various job positions aligned to qualification levels and recognized training centers (see Appendix A, this chapter).

The pathway from the entry management level culminates in the grade of fellow, which BIFM considers should be the aspiration for all within the FM profession. Without further analysis, it is unclear whether this expectation is realistic for those within the profession who are con-tent at an administrative or middle-management level. However, aspects of the fellowship process may be worth emulating in that it provides a general pathway through experience and intense examination (written and oral) to positions of significant influence among the professions associated with the built environment.

Facility Management Association of Australia (FMA Australia)

Established in 1989, the Facility Management Association of Australia (FMA Australia) was an offspring of IFMA of Australia (IFMAA). Viewing itself as the "peak national representative body for the [FM] industry," FMA Australia is similar to other country-based FM associations, yet its core values stress some unique aspects of advocacy, such as contributing to the health and well-being of Australians and the prosperity of the nation, and advancing FM as a profession internationally. This external focus is apparent in its formal advocacy roles in dealing with the govern-ment and regulatory bodies, encouraging the development of university courses in FM, and promoting the FM profession across the boundaries of business, the media, and the wider community.

In a three year (2006–2008) comprehensive national study sanc-tioned by the Ministry of Industry, Tourism, and Resources, FMA Australia partnered with the Australian government and industry repre-sentatives in an ambitious undertaking to raise recognition of the FM industry within the built environment sector, governments, and the wider community. This initiative, the *FM Action Agenda – Managing the Built Environment*, concentrated on four platforms: innovation, education and training, regulatory reform, and sustainability. In regard to education and training, the Agenda working group cited a clearly identified need to ensure that FM is seen as a professional career path in its own right. As part of a broader campaign to raise the profile of the FM profession, the working group delineated a series of actions across the educational spectrum, involving industry, the vocational education sector, and universities. Significant headway has been made, with FM curricula established and growing throughout the educational sector, including extensive programs in academia. Concurrently introduced was an FM profession awareness campaign directed at those who influence career choice. This campaign is integral to sustaining the expansion of the educational programs, and, conversely, the more rooted FM is within university curricula, the more interest is generated in FM careers. There is an extensive compilation on www.FMA.com.au of the FM programs and courses that are part of Australia's "tertiary" educational network.

To its credit, FMA Australia has pursued a strategic approach in elevating the profile of the FM profession, through developing alliances with the government, academia, the vocational education sector, and industry, and it is allied with other partner organizations in global FM, with a particular relationship with BIFM and IFMA through an International Memorandum of Understanding. As part of the IMOU, FMA Australia collaborated with IFMA in adopting the FMP and CFM designations for its members.

European Facility Management Network (EuroFM)

The European Facility Management Network (EuroFM) was founded in the Netherlands in 1993 with the objective of being the "hub of FM research." Research among its 80-plus member organizations, more than half of which are research or educational institutions, is conducted within three network groups: practice, research, and education. The groups conduct research, report out on best practices, and undertake projects such as publishing the *European Facilities Management Education Guide*, a one-stop reference guide for stakeholders across Europe that is intended to bridge the information gap between FM education institutions and industry (EuroFM, 2009). By facilitating the standardization of FM curricula among the many academic member institutions, EuroFM is helping to develop and refine the FM career pipeline.

EuroFM also issues a quarterly electronic-based FM news platform, *European FM Insight* (eFMi), which provides an outlet for critical thinking among the profession's researchers, educators, and practitioners. The platform draws from existing publications through partnership agreements.

The Facilities Society

Founded in 2008, The Facilities Society is a nonprofit that has a strategic alliance with the Facility Management Association (United Kingdom), and it views itself as "dedicated to an interdisciplinary and cross-sector academic enterprise to support the needs of the UK research community, government, businesses, and the public interest." This organization has an uncommon purpose among those noted here, in that its expressed purpose is to bridge the divide between those academic disciplines engaged within the built environment as a distinct sector and those that are working in the community at large, such as healthcare, transportation, commerce, and energy. This kind of vision is what can help elevate FM to be among those professions that are universally recognized as integral to the welfare of society.

Other National FM Associations

A plethora of national FM associations exists in countries and major cities across the world. Denmark, Hong Kong, Korea, Singapore, France, South Africa, Hungary, and Brazil are some examples. These associations provide local networking and programs for members, and many are beginning to provide educational content for members.

Competency Architecture for Credentials

As depicted in Table 2.2, there is commonality among the three prominent global FM professional associations in how they develop their credential programs, yet nuances in emphasis are evident in their respective competency architectures. For each, the architecture drives the development of education and training undergirding the credential programs. The source of this figure, Professor Danny Then, comments that as an applied profession, FM's link between academic (knowledge) and professional (knowledge and practical experience) qualifications requires careful nurturing to be effective.

As the FM profession evolves to meet the increasing complexity of operating the built environment, the professional associations ensure that primary credential requirements keep pace, including a spin-off credential in sustainability, even as specialty trade associations proliferate. Table 2.3 shows a current snapshot of the myriad credentials, offering FM professionals many avenues for mastering complexity and for career development. See Appendix B's glossary (at the end of this chapter) for cross-references to the abbreviations.

As shown in Appendix C, "Framework for Full FM Career Planning" (at the end of this chapter), the profession can be divided into four primary categories, based on job functions, education requirements, credentials,

Table 2.2 Comparison of competency architecture among leading FM associations (Then, 2004)

IFMA	BIFM	FMAA
Facility management is "a profession that encompasses multiple disciplines to ensure functionality of the work environment by integrating people, place, processes and technology."	Facility management is "the integration of multidisciplinary activities within the built environment and the management of their impact upon people and the workplace."	Facility management is "a business practice that optimizes people, process, assets, and the work environment to support the delivery of an organization's business objectives."
Core competencies	**Core competencies**	**Competency standards**
Leadership and management	Understanding business organizations	Use organizational understanding too manage facilities
Human and environmental factors	Managing people	Develop strategic facility response
Planning and project management	Managing premises	Manage risk
Operations and maintenance	Managing services	Manage facility portfolio
Finance	Managing the work environment	Improve facility performance
Real estate	Managing resources	Manage the delivery of services
Communication		Manage projects
Quality assessment and innovation		Manage financial performance
Technology		Arrange and implement procurement/ sourcing
		Facilitate communication
		Manage workplace relationships
		Manage change
Focus	**Focus**	**Focus**
Multidisciplinary profession	Multidisciplinary activities	Driven by business objectives
Functionality of the work environment	Relationship between built environment and workplace	Coordinating management function
Integration of resources (people, place, and technology) and processes	Relationship between people and the workplace	Supporting business function

Table 2.3 Matrix of credentials of US-based professional associations

Professional association	Technician	FM professional	FM manager	Executive	Specialty
IFMA	FMP	FMP	CFM		SFP
APPA		EFP	CEFP	Fellow	
CoreNet			MCR	SLCR	
BOMA	SMT/SMA	FMA	RPA		
AHA		CHC	CHFM		
IREM			CPM		
IAMC				Fellow	
PRSMA		RFMP			
IAAM			CFE		
SMRP		CMRP			
AFE		CPS	CPMM		CPE
USGBC					LEED AP
ASHRAE		OPMP			
AEE					CEM
PMI					PMP

and experience. While a career ladder may progress from the technical to the executive level, there is a strong contingent of midlevel technicians, professionals, and managers currently in the FM field. Many of these professionals may not aspire to senior executive status, but they need guidance to enhance and expand their impact within their current category of technician, professional, or manager. Senior FM executives would have a viewpoint primarily focused on business (organizational) issues that are heavily concentrated in finance, marketing, and development.

Alignment of CCET with Industry

The FM profession as a whole recognizes the imperative for aligning in its entirety with the goals of the enterprise. To effectively do this requires developing and exploiting the intellectual capital within the profession through the CCET apparatus of institutional stakeholders. Over the past decade, credential and continuing education programs and networking within the profession have progressed to a superior level, comparable even with those of established traditional professions, including the ancillary FM professions such as design and engineering.

Yet, industry by and large still relegates FM to a peripheral role or even as an afterthought when it comes to strategy. And this condition may become entrenched as highly experienced FM leaders in the baby boomer generation retire in droves.

Consequently, a gap in experience and associated competency is looming, just when more advanced expertise is required to meet the proliferating and juxtaposed demands of aging and ultramodern structures within the built environment. With the pipeline starved of talent, the growing focus on life-cycle sustainability may sputter and lose momentum.

Assimilation and exploitation of talent are constricted throughout the pipeline, impacting the FM profession's competency levels globally. Access to the profession is vague or asymmetrical for college graduates and midcareer cross-overs. The lagging element within the CCET apparatus is the role of academia in accelerating the replenishment of the talent pipeline and in advancing the expertise and credibility of executives within the FM community. The long-term welfare of the profession is in the strategic application of higher education (i.e. as FM and CRE degrees become more prevalent, the C-suite will take notice). This will pave the way for major profession status while developing interest and expertise within the next generation.

Conventional wisdom and evidence among FM professionals are that most learning stems from reading reference materials, performing Internet research, networking among peers, and taking short-duration courses and seminars. Apparently, the professional associations are so adept at what they offer in the way of training programs, symposia, and body of knowledge research that many within the profession are quite content with a "tactical and practical" approach to professional enrichment, and are unwilling to invest the time, effort, or money to undertake studies through higher education.

The conundrum for FM professional associations, industry, and academia is how to align on setting a vision for a broad-based educational network of degree programs. Industry perpetuates the common view of FM as focused on operational support and a catch-all for non-core functions and services. In turn, the FM professional associations may actually reinforce this view by designing their extensive repertoire of training seminars and symposia to accommodate industry's desire for FM to be highly proficient, cost savvy, and excellent in delivery of services.

Because of this competency-based training focus, the demand for higher education in both luring young people into the profession and developing thought leaders for the profession is relatively low. Industry trails rather than leads not only in advising on curricula development but also in expanding accredited degree programs throughout the university system. The reasons for this are manifold, but industry consensus views FM as composed of practitioners, essential to day-to-day operations, rather than business leaders possessing the formal education and associated status of a traditional profession. Further, those who enter the profession through the few undergraduate programs tend to be incidental in matriculation and even geography by way of proximity to the university offering FM degrees. In addition to the perception that the pathway to the FM profession is ill defined, Badger and Garvin (2007) said that "little university and private research information exists in the field of facilities asset management and even less research funding is being introduced or implemented."

The missing link to altering this perception is between higher education and industry, by determining what roles academia can play in order to equip industry with a new generation of FM professionals who can pivot between the tactical and strategic, with the latter role as dominant. The professional associations such as IFMA should be the linchpin to connecting this linkage. Associations have focused on early to midcareer professionals and managers, accommodating their need for practical training. As noted here, without prevalent and widespread participation in higher education programs, the mind-set will default to tactical.

So, how can the FM profession catapult itself to the heights of strategic relevance? First, convene a standing task force of CCET stakeholders among the professional associations, industry, and academia to develop a roadmap for inquiry and direction. As a prerequisite, this is no easy task itself, and the term *task* may be a misnomer as it will be necessary to take the long view in devising a strategic CCET renewal plan for the profession. Also, the stakeholders are multitudinous and may have divergent agendas. Therefore, the task force should be composed of top FM or CRE executives and subject matter experts in varied sectors of industry, government, professional associations, and higher education. Once established, the task force should undertake a study of transformational strategies, as discussed in the "Paradigm of Sequence" section.

Paradigm of Sequence and Emphasis on Education versus Training

Examine and emulate affiliate professions working within the built environment sector that are considered top-tier professions, including architecture, engineering, and law (real estate and construction). In these professions, university study is the entry point, then specialization (usually graduate school), and then licensing (permission to practice at an advanced level). This orientation assures a steady infusion of talent, a rigorous testing ground throughout the period of formal education (while attrition assures a committed base of talent), and more formal credentials (licensing through written and oral examination) aimed toward legitimate practice within the profession. In the FM profession, academic qualification is unspecified, and credentialing is positioned at the forefront of the process for professional recognition, hence the concentration on short-term practical training in seminars, symposia, and classes, including intense prepping for credential exams.

To shift precedence from practical training to formal university instruction will require extensive groundwork, even a seismic change. Although there are some strong accredited undergraduate and graduate school programs offering courses of study in FM, they are sparse in number (see Appendix A, this chapter, for a list of programs in North America and the rest of the world). To accelerate the paradigm shift, the task force may consider concurrent horizontal and vertical development strategies following these principles:

- *Proliferate*: Focus on major metropolitan areas to partner with industry to entreat public universities to develop FM certificate and continuing education programs at institutions with no FM education.
- *One-up*: At higher education institutions with only a certificate FM or undergraduate program, provide an incremental approach to develop curricula pointing toward the next level of degree.
- *Diversify*: Pursue variations within higher education that could support the FM profession even more, such as formal dual degrees (e.g. MBA, law, and engineering), continuing education for seasoned professionals, thought leadership forums hosted by universities, and more juried publication research to help codify best practices in leadership.
- *Bottom-up*: There must be emphasis on front-line leadership skills by targeting community colleges and vocational technical schools to incorporate certificate and associate FM degree programs. FM leadership cannot attain strategic relevance unless the foundation of technical skills is intact.

These strategies require a vision propelled by newfound partnerships, underwriting, campaigning, branding, and perseverance.

Framework of FM Competence – Leaning Forward to the Enterprise

Vital to this transformation is orienting the FM competence architecture toward enterprise alignment; otherwise, industry will remain ambivalent in its support of the FM profession as part of its strategy. As alignment becomes more precise, the FM profession is more inclined to import ideas and technologies by intensively developing formal research mechanisms in support of the competency architecture for the workforce of the future.

Enterprise Alignment with the Life Cycle of Talent

As the competency architecture aligns with the enterprise's goals, and the associated CCET framework repositions higher education influence in bolstering the profession, the talent pipeline will prosper. Analogous to the life cycle of physical assets, talent will have a formal inception in undergraduate professional education, mature through stages nurtured by competency-based training elements leading to certification, accelerate through graduate-level continuing education and advanced credentials, and end in positions of thought leadership. As the talent strategy is under-girded by a robust CCET framework with FM career education majors as a cornerstone, the profession will attain recognition as a major discipline. Other ways to enhance profession status may include the following:

- Identify barriers to recruitment among university students, and develop a standardized program kit for FM professional association chapters to participate in career fairs. Devise a profile of leadership characteristics, aptitude, and education, and then pinpoint high-potential students for chapter membership scholarships.
- Seed the profession with midcareer cross-overs. As noted in this chapter, many have entered the FM profession this way, but such entry tends to be opportunistic and incidental. Develop guidelines and profiles to actively recruit such individuals. Professional associations should tailor road show seminars to attract cross-overs and provide guidance to the industry on internal recruitment (e.g. mini-sabbaticals for candidates).
- Recast career streams to focus on accession from universities and cross-overs.
- Establish and measure benchmarks for recruitment, and incorporate them into each professional association's strategic plans.
- Conduct and publish more studies on the long-term prospects of the FM profession, such as the one conducted by Arizona State University (Sullivan *et al.*, 2010).
- Begin a systematic approach to alliance building with specialty FM professional associations. Enlist FM professional association councils to help develop the strategy for initiating alliances, including sharing of products and services, ad hoc participation among each other's Boards of Directors and Councils, and advocacy initiatives on government standards and issues. Although this could begin as an emulation of the EuroFM or Global FM models, the long-range goal should ultimately point toward consolidation. Within the alliances, work with industry on competency profiles and develop recruitment strategies. With the baby boomer generation lurching toward retirement, addressing the critical staffing shortfall should be a common cause across the profession.
- Develop an online catalog that organizes and links all available FM products and services, university programs, knowledge centers, and online communities.
- Convene a joint association task committee to devise a common set of competencies, create an FM CCET framework crossing the spectrum of FM position levels, and provide guidance on technical and managerial career ladder options.

- Convene a joint association task committee on academic affairs, seeking to make foundational inroads to the academy in undergraduate, graduate, and professional development programs.
- Convene a joint association task committee to develop research centers of excellence for FM practitioners and to evaluate the BOK within each FM professional association, with an eye toward a common and comprehensive FM BOK.
- Convene a joint association task committee to evaluate credential systems, looking for synergies such as formal acceptance of continuing education from other associations, studying licensure models, and setting up a credential committee (composed of national and local leadership) to orally examine candidates.
- Create executive-level credentials and associated thought leader forums within the major professional associations.
- Devise a formal system for thought leader series, leadership councils, credentials, and the application pathway to Fellow status.
- Examine how the IFMA Foundation can expand its influence to other FM associations.
- Educate members on peer-reviewed journals.
- Create a culture within the profession to encourage senior leaders to publish peer-reviewed articles, moderate forums and panels, regularly meet with other senior leaders, and pursue executive continuing education.
- Commission case studies of fourth-generation integrated outsourcing's intent to nurture the FM strategist who delegates the base business of operations to integrators.
- Propagate the concept of a Chief Facility Executive by profiling the FM executive as a strategist (Barnes, 2010). This concept can be the catalyst to transforming the profession, so it is explored in further detail in the "Framing CCET" section.

Framing CCET to Produce the Next Generation of FM and CRE Strategic Thinkers

For those seeking a career path culminating in the executive level of FM, the trajectory can be variegated, giving the impression that there is no pattern to emulate in terms of experiences, training, education, or achievement. Worse, one may conclude that FM executives attained their level of achievement solely through extraordinary talent, luck, favoritism, or some combination thereof. Yet careful examination of FM executive profiles will reveal patterns of career aspiration planning, opportunistic outlook for leadership experiences that develop character, and pursuit of challenging education and training programs and related credentials.

As noted in this chapter, FM professionals and managers have multiple pathways of preparation and advancement through college,

FM professional associations, and continuing education products and services. When aligned to an aspiration, these products and services can be the catalysts to advancement to senior positions. Typically, the higher the level and size of the organization, the more general the FM position, although there is some latitude for specialization in function (e.g. sustainability, real estate, or construction) or industry (i.e. as noted in this chapter by the many specialty professional associations and credentials).

With the accelerating complexity within the built environment, it is tempting to specialize within the FM career field. And given the regulatory and liability pitfalls, some senior FM executive specialists are necessary. Yet, most positions within the C-suite face the same challenge of producing the generalist leader, capable of decisiveness across a complex spectrum of responsibilities, and this is no less so with the FM executive. The larger risk within the FM community is that, unlike other well-developed professions, FM tends to be a catch-all for noncore services classified as "support" or "service," which diminishes FM's strategic orientation and contributions to the business. Although IFMA and its global partners are the dominant FM professional associations, perhaps inhibiting the enterprise view is the loose or even fragmented federation of specialty associations within the profession, as noted in this chapter.

Although there is no formulaic approach to reaching the senior executive levels within the FM profession, there is a mainstream pathway that enhances the chance of attaining this. IFMA provides that pathway to technical and/or middle management with the CFM credential and related training, and for beyond that, there are senior executive opportunities in speaking at symposia and conferences, in chapter leadership, and in contributing to publications. However, the products and services are less defined for the FM executive sustaining his or her position as a thought leader within business and the FM profession itself; this is an area where the FM professional associations, including IFMA, fall short, primarily due to the fragmentation of specialties and the bias toward middle-management technical and service competencies in training and credentials. There are, however, examples within the various professional associations of products and services targeting the senior executive:

- In addition to its primary competence credential (MCR), CoreNet offers an executive-level credential, the Senior Leader Corporate Real Estate (SLCR), which is attained by attending a series of thought leader forums.
- APPA, IAMC, and BIFM offer a pathway to apply for Fellow status with an emphasis on leadership and professional accomplishment in addition to professional association service leadership activities, and therefore there is perhaps more incentive to attain this status than through nomination only.

- Some associations offer thought leader panels, advisory council positions, or symposia.

Finally, although relatively uncommon, there are some FM executives who are actually a member of the C-suite or at least have a seat at the table in the Boardroom. Barnes (2010) studied the concept of the "Chief Facility Executive" and determined several personal attributes or organizational strategies for this executive, related to external focus, enterprise alignment, global strategy, high finance acumen, intellectual capital, organizational design, and marketing of FM. The FM or CRE professional as a polymath, well versed in and outside of the profession, can be a role model as an executive by taking advantage of opportunities such as adjunct professorships, publishing articles in trade journals, engaging politicians and economic development experts, working with internal communications to position FM or CRE initiatives with the media, participating in community events, understanding and demonstrating strong leadership in sustainability, developing global insights, and so on. These critical success factors and stronger linkage among professional associations would help elevate the profile of the FM profession as well as the senior executives within the profession.

Summary and Conclusions

In contrast to established professions such as medicine, law, architecture, public accounting, and professional engineering, there are no standard prerequisite qualifications for practicing FM. This is all the more reason to have in place a dynamic framework of competencies that is sustained through progressive education, training, and development of facility managers that recognize different needs across the spectrum of management levels, from the FM professional to the senior executive (Clark and Hinxman, 1999).

Because of the multitude of specialty FM professional associations and disparate products and services, including training programs and credentials, the FM CCET framework, while strong up through the facility manager level, is disjointed in providing aspirational guidance to professionals seeking FM executive positions (i.e. those within the highest levels of the organization).

> Although the learning and credential programs of the professional associations have been the cornerstones for competence, the growing importance of degree and continuing education programs in academia provides a means to deepen the external credibility of FM as a major profession.

Taking a holistic and global perspective of FM career management may strengthen the FM CCET framework and thereby elevate the profile of the profession, perhaps emulating aspects of the traditional professions.

References

Association of Higher Education Facilities Officers (APPA). (2002). *Development of the facility management profession*. Alexandria, VA: APPA.

Badger, W.W., and Garvin, M.J. (2007). Facilities asset management: challenges and opportunities. Paper presented at the 25th CME Conference, University of Reading, UK, 14–17 July.

Barnes, R. (2010). Concept of chief facility executive. *International Journal of Facility Management*. 1 (1).

Clark, E., and Hinxman L. (1999). Developing a framework of competencies for facilities management. *Facilities*. 17 (7/8), 246–252.

Dohner, R. (2004). Corporate real estate management: a profession? *Journal of Corporate Real Estate*, 6 (3), 200–203.

European Facility Management Network. (2009). *European facilities management education guide*. Available at: http://www.eurofm.org/library/education-guide-2009/ (accessed 4 July 2013).

Jensen, P.A. (2010). The facilities management value map: a conceptual network. *Facilities*. 28 (3/4), 175–188.

Sullivan, K., Georgoulis, S., and Lines, B. (2010). Empirical study of the current United States facilities management profession. *Journal of Facilities Management*. 8 (2), 91–103.

Then, D. (2004). The future of professional facility management education in the Asia-Pacific region. Paper presented at the New World Order of Facility Management conference, Hong Kong.

Waheed, Z., and Fernie, S. (2009). Knowledge based facilities management. *Facilities*. 27 (7/8), 258–266.

Appendix A: Accredited Degree Programs

The International Facility Management Association (IFMA) Foundation is the accrediting body for facility management (FM) programs internationally. Standards of Accreditation can be found at the IFMA Foundation website: http://www.ifmafoundation.org/scholarships/standards.pdf.

The following are current IFMA Foundation Accredited Programs:

North America

Bachelor's Degree Programs

Brigham Young University, Provo, UT, offers a BS degree in Facilities Management with a Business Management minor from the national accredited Marriott School of Management through the College of Engineering and Technology in the School of Technology Facilities Management. http://www.byu.edu/webapp/home/index.jsp.

Conestoga College Institute of Technology and Advanced Learning, Kitchener, ON, Canada offers a Bachelor's degree in Project and Facility Management. http://www.conestogac.on.ca.

Cornell University, Ithaca, NY, offers a BS and MS degree in Facilities Management. The programs are offered through the New York State College of Human Ecology. http://www.cornell.edu.

Ferris State University, Big Rapids, MI, offers a BS degree program and an online Certificate program in Facility Management through the College of Engineering Technology.

Wentworth Institute of Technology, Boston, MA, offers a BS in Facilities Planning and Management through the Department of Design and Facilities.

Master's Degree Programs

Georgia Institute of Technology (Georgia Tech), Atlanta, GA, offers a MS in Building Construction and Integrated Facility Management through the College of Architecture, School of Building Construction. http://www.gatech.edu.

Pratt Institute, Manhattan, New York, NY, offers an MS degree in Facilities Management through the School of Architecture, Department of Facilities Management. http://www.pratt.edu.

Europe

Bachelor's Degree Programs

FH Kufstein, Tirol, Austria, offers a Magister (FH) for Facility Management. http://www.fh-kufstein.ac.at/wi/jluethi/research_e.html.

Hanze University Groningen, The Netherlands, offers a Bachelor's degree program in Facilities Management through the School of Facility Management, in an international environment. http://www.hanze.nl/home/International.

NHTV Breda University of Applied Science, Breda, The Netherlands, offers a degree in Facility Management. http://www.nhtv.nl/default.aspx?themaset=c910a88f-0245-4d9e-b847-4dd2ebc0e2a7.

Saxion Universities of Applied Sciences, Deventer, The Netherlands, offers a Bachelor's degree in Facility Management. http://www.saxion.nl.

Master's Degree Programs

Leeds Metropolitan University Leeds, UK, offers a web-based distance-learning MSC in Facilities Management through the School of the Built Environment. This can be studied off-campus worldwide. http://www.lmu.ac.uk/

Asia

Master's Degree Program

The Hong Kong Polytechnic University, Hung Hom, Kowloon, Hong Kong, offers a Graduate Program in Facility Management. http://www.polyu.edu.hk/cpa/polyu/main/main_e.php.

Appendix B: Facility Management (FM) Organizations

FM Resource Organizations

American Institute of Architects (AIA)
American Society of Heating, Refrigerating and Air-Conditioning Engineers (ASHRAE)
APPA: Leadership in Educational Facilities
ASIS International
Association for Facilities Engineering (AFE)
Association of Energy Engineers (AEE)
Building Owners and Managers Association (BOMA) International
Building Owners and Managers Institute (BOMI) International
CoreNet Global
Counselors of Real Estate (CRE)
Institute of Real Estate Management (IREM)
International Facility Management Association (IFMA)
ISSA, The Worldwide Cleaning Industry Association
Society for College and University Planning (SCUP)
Society of Industrial and Office Realtors (SIOR)
US Green Building Council (USGBC)

International FM Organizations

Associação Brasileira de Facilities (ABRAFAC) – Brazil
Association des Directeurs et Responsables de Services Généraux (ARSEG) – France
British Institute of Facilities Management (BIFM) – United Kingdom
European Facility Management Network (EuroFM) – Europe/ The Netherlands

Facilities Management Association of New Zealand (FMANZ) – New Zealand

Facility Management Association of Australia (FMA Australia) – Australia

German Facility Management Association (GEFMA) – Germany

Global Facility Management Association (Global FM) – International/Belgium

Hong Kong Institute of Facility Management (HKIFM) – Hong Kong

Hungarian Facility Management Society (HFMS) – Hungary

Japan Facility Management Promotion Association (JFMA) – Japan

Property Institute of New Zealand (PINZ) – New Zealand

Der Schweizer Facility Management Verein (FM-ARENA) – Switzerland

South African Facilities Management Association (SAFMA) – South Africa

Appendix C: Framework for Full FM Career Planning

FM career framework

Job level	Position	Qualifications	Knowledge and skills	Trade association	Credential
Technician	**CAD analyst**	CAD software (2D or 3D), drafting, design, and advanced computer skills.	Mechanical aptitude, abstract visualization, math, and blueprint reading.	BOMA	SMT
	Electrician	Varies by state code; can include apprenticeships.	Mechanical aptitude and drawing, applied physics and chemistry, shop math, electronics, blueprint reading, and computer software and applications.	BOMA, local unions	SMT
	HVAC mechanic	Varies by state code; some require a license; can include apprenticeships.	Shop math, mechanical drawing, applied physics and chemistry, electronics, blueprint reading, and computer applications.	ASHRAE, NCCER, HVAC Excellence, PAHRA, NADCA	HVACR programs
	BAS administrator	Varies by BAS application (e.g. JCI Metasys, Siemens Apogee, Honeywell, and Trane)	Mechanical aptitude and drawing, applied physics and chemistry, shop math, electronics, blueprint reading, and computer software and applications.	BOMA	SMA
	CMMS coordinator	Varies by CMMS (e.g. Maximo, SAP, and MP2)	Blueprint reading, and computer software and applications, math, architectural drawing.	BOMA	SMA
	Central plant operator	Training in plant operations.	Basic mechanical and HVAC operations knowledge and problem-solving abilities.	ASHRAE	

	Plumber	Varies by state code; can include apprenticeships.	Shop math, mechanical drawing, applied physics and chemistry, electronics, blueprint reading, and computer applications.	Local unions and apprenticeship programs	
FM professional	**Maintenance supervisor**	Three or more years of experience and supervisory training.	Maintenance & Operations knowledge with supervisory skills training or experience.	SMRP	CMRP
	Custodial services supervisor		Thorough understanding of cleaning, janitorial and supervisory skills. Second language often required.	IFMA	FMP
	Space planner	Previous commercial interior design or FM experience; knowledge of specialized computer applications used in the field, including AutoCAD.	Logical and analytic thinker, detail-oriented, blueprint reading, computer applications, ability to analyze space utilization and facilities inventory and make recommendations for optimal usage.	IFMA, JDA	FMP, SPC, SPPC
	Construction project administrator	Degree in construction administration or management, or civil engineering.	Logical and analytic thinker, detail-oriented, blueprint reading, computer applications, ability to schedules, budget and project control, estimating and negotiation skills.	PMI, CMAA	PMP
	Security services supervisor	Security services experience and education (BA in security services)	Good supervisory and communication skills; dependable employee; security-awareness.	IFMA or BOMA ASIS international	FMP, PSP

(Continued)

FM career framework

Job level	Position	Qualifications	Knowledge and skills	Trade association	Credential
	Energy engineer	Familiarity with state-of-the-art energy systems and energy savings benefits; engineering degree or equivalent experience.	Mechanical aptitude, skilled in energy auditing, energy modeling and simulation, computer applications, blueprint reading.	AFE, ASHRAE, USGBC	CPS, OPMP, LEED AP
FM manager	**Operations manager**	College degree generally required, with 5 or more years of experience in one or more specialization and 3 or more years of supervisory experience; certification(s) may be required.	Function specific requirements in each job may vary, basic experience and knowledge in specialization, along with ability to manage staff, customers and develop productivity, financial, and other reports to senior management.	IFMA or BOMA	CFM or RPA
	Project manager			IFMA, PMI	CFM, PMP
	Facility manager			IFMA or BOMA	CFM, LEED AP
	Planning manager			IFMA, CoreNet	CFM, MCR
	Engineering manager			AFE, AEE	CPMM, CEM or LEED AP
	Administrative services manager			IFMA or BOMA	CFM
	Physical plant manager			AFE, AEE	CPMM, CEM
FM executive	**Director executive Director Vice president Chief facility officer**	Demonstrated success in leadership roles.	Business acumen, risk orientation, and innovative mind-set.	Two or more of the following: IFMA, CoreNet, BOMA, Urban Land Institute, and a specialty FM association.	Fellow or equivalent (e.g. SLCR) in at least one of the mainstream trade associations.

FM Consultancy and Client–Provider Relationships

Kathy O. Roper

Georgia Institute of Technology, Atlanta, GA

Managing professional practice in facility management (FM) requires an unusually broad balance of activities. Balance of sales, with technical expertise, human resource management and also the important component of relationships, make the professional practice of FM one of the most precarious, yet rewarding, practices.

FM as defined by numerous associations and experts includes a broad scope of services to benefit an organisation's workforce and supports the primary objectives of the organisation. These services normally range from strategic planning for workspace needs to real estate transactions; operational maintenance of workspaces; mail, reprographic and other administrative services; as well as constant updates to the organisation's workspaces to keep them organisationally appropriate and functional as rapidly changing organisations transform and innovate. The International Facility Management Association (IFMA) defines FM as "a profession that encompasses multiple disciplines to ensure functionality of the built environment by integrating people, place, process and technology." This broad range of potential services is one area of primary importance and potential failure for FM practices.

Historically, FM professional practices sprung from one primary area of expertise. As the acceptance of outsourcing expanded and corporate

This chapter is an authorized reprint from the 2011 book *Managing the Professional Practice in the Built Environment*, Chapter 8, originally titled "How Thin to Win: FM Service Provision Issues," edited by Hedley Smyth and published by Wiley-Blackwell.

users sought single-source or all-in-one providers, many professional service providers expanded their offerings and services. Ikon, a copier and printing organisation, provided expertise in outsourced reprographic services. Their expansion into mail, shipping and other document services led to their current business as "document management strategists," addressing a full range of document planning and services. Jones, Lang, LaSalle began business as a Chicago real estate brokerage company and is now a global property, investment, energy-planning and project management service organisation. Johnson Controls, which began business as a room thermostat manufacturer, now provides services in automotive interiors, building efficiency and power solutions.

The desire to be everything to everyone is a tempting yet impossible business model. Thoughtful professional practices recognise their limitations, and many have focused on limited services in which they can provide true expertise and value. The way in which firms choose to limit their scope, as indicated by the examples of Ikon, Johnson Controls and Jones, Lang, LaSalle, differentiates their offers and appeal to particular customers and market segments. Even when considering the maturation of outsourcing practices over the last decade, primary business issues remain that are difficult and recurring in today's FM professional practice. Three of these are addressed in the remainder of this chapter:

- Client–contractor relationships
- Minimizing costs while maximizing value, or "how thin to win" the bid
- Managing scope creep while maintaining a customer service orientation.

Client–Contractor Relationships

Essential to any good contractual relationship is the "fit" of the parties in the relationship. As shown in Figure 3.1, the relationship between the client-user and the professional service provider is the most critical and essential consideration of any contract for professional FM services. The scope and key performance indicators (KPIs) of every contract are important, but most procurement processes have developed these to fine detail. Price is, of course, an important consideration, but even outside the boundaries of the legal contract, the relationship of the client and the contractor has major impacts. Before procurement processes begin, the reputation, image, recognition as well as financial stability of the professional FM practice are paramount. Many requests for proposals (RFPs) will be sent to only well-known organisations, requiring successful bidders to have a background and track record of quality. For this reason, it is often difficult for start-up organisations to gain clients without a privileged opening or market entry to provide the first client introduction or experience. Start-ups in FM, as shown in

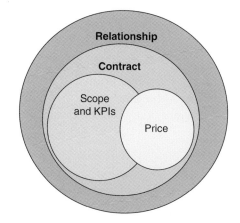

Figure 3.1   Professional practice framework.

historical experience, start small and grow their business over time, gaining credibility and recognition as they expand.

The importance of the client–contractor relationship is often under-evaluated or even overlooked in traditional procurement practices. Especially in public sector organisations with procurement regulations emphasising low-price competitive bidding, the value of positive relationships is not easily quantified. Unfortunately, these people issues have been known to overshadow even otherwise good contracts, often resulting in legal wrangling to dissolve or renegotiate unhappy relationships.

It is often difficult to even get in front of the busy FM executive to discuss the potential offered by professional FM practices. They often view the opportunity as "another thing to manage" – another thing under which they are "drowning" – and for this reason, they particularly need the help and expertise offered. The most reliable method is to build an environment of trust in their busy environment. Sending a short article related to their specific organisational need might be a step to demonstrate expertise and goodwill. The article may not relate directly to your service but demonstrates that you take the time and trouble to understand clients and have their improvement in mind. Often, internal facility managers are penalised by their management for not doing a good enough job, and these managers face fear of losing their position, when, in fact, the ability to turn over (parts of) the service via a contract to an expert who can provide the best job may save this manager's reputation and job within the organisation. Helping the client reach this understanding without another office visit or time away from his or her schedule may be possible with a good reputation, appropriate advertising and timely low-key contact as provided in the example of the article. The goal of the professional provider is to establish trust and build on this during business development in order that the potential client participates positively in specifying portions of the service content, based on your service offer, and the client then goes on to lever a more finely tuned and demanding service out of the contract agreement and throughout the service period. This is a form of co-created value that secures business and competitive advantage directly for the professional practice and indirectly for the client (Prahalad and Ramaswamy, 2004a,b).

While all the influences upon the relationship are not shown in Figure 3.1, there are many that exist and should be considered.

The major impact of the relationship and alignment of similar values and expectations is known as "fit." This term is also used in traditional human resource hiring, such that the objective of finding the correct attitude, values as well as experience and expertise is considered when bringing someone new into the organisation. This is even more important when a contract organisation joins with the core organisation to provide services, since numerous personnel typically fulfil the contract and they must all meet similar guidelines for how to work with the customer organisation in order to be successful in this area of aligning attitudes, values and expectations.

While employees of the contract provider are required to conform to the professional values and standards of their organisation, they must also be "client facing," that is, flexible enough to align with the client's organisational norms, which should be possible with a reasonable inter-organisational "fit."

Inter-organisational relationships, those between two or more separate organisations, have been studied by Ring and Van de Ven (1994) and described as "socially contrived mechanisms for collective action, which are continually shaped and restructured by actions and symbolic interpretations of the parties involved" (p. 96). When positive relationships can be established, typically additional work, extensions of contracts and successful rebids are frequent. Negative relationships almost always end in non-renewed and terminated contracts, even when savings are demonstrated. Ring and Van de Ven discussed a concept of "actions and symbolic interpretations," which can be demonstrated with a positive example of a contractor with values similar to those of the core organisation, who comes into the client organisation with staff who have cheerful, upbeat attitudes, and this positive relationship results in customers who notice the positive attitude and view their delivery of service as more positive in satisfaction surveys. A negative example of the symbolic interpretation would be a new provider who did not live up to the previously provided level of customer service and was defensive when questioned about it; this provider's results in customer satisfaction surveys showed poor scores and a decline in the satisfaction level overall from the facility service organisation.

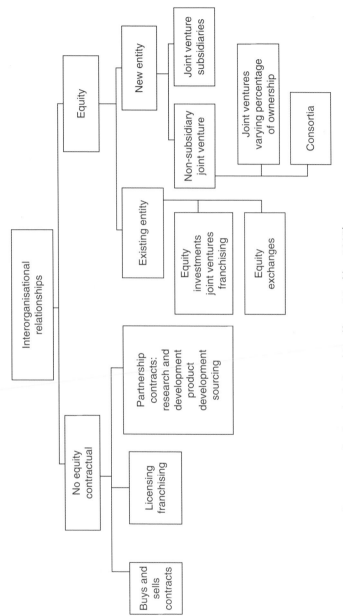

Figure 3.2 Types of inter-organisational relationships (from Mockler, 1997).

Obviously, all people are different and exhibit their unique personality in each situation, but for service organisations, the leadership expectations and examples set by managers can strongly influence and model the expected behaviours that align with customer values and expectations. The best providers have a high level of training and expectations for their staff, and their own values often may be higher and more positive than required. This is an important area of best value contracting that performance-based contracts can deliver. Giving the provider the ability to innovate and improve service delivery, and incentivising these improvements, provides positive actions and symbolic interpretations of the parties for mutual benefit.

There are multiple settings for inter-organisational relationships that can be developed, from a simple purchase or buy-sell contract, through various equity position ventures or exchanges. Several of these are outlined in Figure 3.2, which is adapted from work in the mid-1990s by Mockler (1997). Moving from the left of the figure, with small or larger, long-term, buy-sell contracts to equity partnership and joint ventures, this figure illustrates that many different structures exist for working with outside organisations. For long-term services, some organisations have found that an entirely new entity, formed in partnership with former customers and providers, may provide a more stable, profitable structure for all. An example of such a new entity would be the spin-off of specific service functions, for example space reconfiguration planning and implementation from the imaginary JCN Company's in-house staff, into a joint venture company. This new company is composed of the employees of JCN, who formerly planned and implemented these reconfigurations, with the ABC furniture moving organisation with expertise in cubicle installation and handling, so that both organisations become more expert in their core areas, and the new company has an immediate opening or opportunity with the JCN core company. In the early days of outsourcing, this was not an uncommon type of relationship, rather than the purchase of the services from the ABC furniture company and the subsequent dilemma of how to handle the in-house staff during and after the new contract. The new entity or company arrangement frees both JCN and ABC to focus on their expertise, and the new entity begins with experienced staff but sets its own mission and objectives, while retaining the values of employees who moved from JCN and merged with the expertise of ABC.

It may be helpful to remember the suggestion of Franklin (1997) that outsourcing requires a double-prong approach, which values both an economic approach and a behavioural approach. The economic approach requires the practice to clearly understand its strategy from the economic basis and equally address the behavioural approach, including "commitment, persistence, knowledge, pride and interpersonal qualities of an organization's people" (Franklin, 1997, p. 373), when determining strategy. A sole focus on either one can result in deficiencies that may not be easily overcome, and that can synergistically reinforce each other when addressed in tandem.

Summarily, two popular quotes come to mind as advice for maximizing client relationships. Business consultant and academic Michael Porter curtly reminds us, "It's relationships, stupid!" in his book *Competitive Advantage* (1985). And advice to help with adjusting our relationship expectations is prompted by biologist and evolutionist Charles Darwin: it is not the strongest of the species that survives, or the most intelligent, but the one most responsive to change. Despite the range of possible organisational decisions enabling best value service opportunities, and despite inspiring advice, cost always remains a factor that dominates and frequently dictates how FM professional practices compete.

Minimizing Costs While Maximizing Value

The essential charge for any FM organisation is to maximize value to the client organisation and minimize or eliminate costs where reasonable. With in-house FM, this is always a challenge, but with professional practices, it is the life or death of the organisation balance.

In order to cover all business costs, each advisory and service contract must be appropriately bid in order to not only cover all costs but also provide for profit so that the organisation can sustain itself. With competition at its toughest during economic crises, one FM service provider, Gary Merrow (personal communication, August 16, 2009), commented during the credit crunch, "It's all about understanding how thin to win you can become."

As FM clients become more focused on costs, this thin margin of profitability is often comparable to walking a razor's edge. Not only are FM providers forced to second-guess competitor bids, but also they must maintain their margin and not dip below actual costs to survive, on the one hand, and meet customer specifications and expectations, on the other hand. This can become a contentious situation, especially where there is scope creep. During periods of recession, many professional practices look to secure a client with a flat (small- or no-profit) bid for the first few years, expecting to discover innovations and efficiencies during these years that can enhance profits during the longer range years of the contract. Another strategy is to align services for a client so that shortages in one area can be covered by increased profit in other areas. However, this is somewhat dangerous if clients are required or expect to change allocation of work in multiple areas over the course of the contract, potentially leading to the profitable area to shrink and/or the flat, unprofitable areas to expand.

A similar and more risky strategy has been to organise so that clients with flat profit margins are cross-subsidised from more profitable clients – cover annual overheads first, and then seek (premium) profits. But with credit crunch cutbacks, such as those seen in banking, housing, automotive and leisure and travel, this invokes contentious and thus costly relations, contractual disputes, renegotiated contracts and a loss of business for professional practices. Each practice must determine its own risk potential and attempt mitigations to address major risks. Obvious measures for new contracts include avoiding known risky industries, avoiding financially weak clients and clients with adverse reputations, withdrawing bids for potentially unprofitable clients (usually those with high leverage) and not responding to requests that could not become profitable. Such features are not unusual in today's marketplace.

Other strategies that can mitigate potential risks to profits include forming alliances or partnering agreements with existing maintenance providers, especially for specialised equipment, so that both partners share the risk and profit from one client. It may also open up new market segments and potential for bidding for larger consultancy and service provision contracts than would otherwise be the case. Some FM professional services offer these alliances as a benefit of their service. Clients often view it as an expansion of services, and it aids them in reaching the single point of contact (SPOC) they often seek in order to minimize contract management. For a few types of specialised practice, the economic downturn has provided a growth opportunity. Take, for example, the relocation or reconfiguration management sector within a FM practice. As organisations cut staff and limit real estate transactions, these organisations are faced with increased move, add and change (MAC) activity. Other organisations are taking advantage of reduced real estate costs and relocating to less expensive space, creating growth for project managers, movers and other related specialists. With limited staff, these one-off projects provide opportunities that did not exist at this level in a more stable market.

In the United States, where most government contracts favour minority and small-business contracts to meet specific guidelines or quotas, strategic alliances with these smaller practices is a good way to share in gaining access to, and competitive opportunities with, governmental organisations. It also meets the intended purpose in helping to educate and provide experience for these smaller firms as they interact with larger, more established providers. However, competitive realities have resulted in many smaller firms being swallowed up in acquisitions by the larger practices, reducing the competition in many locations to only the big, major companies, whose strategies are based around building market share in recession periods to favourably position themselves during the subsequent upturn.

Another current and important issue for any organisation, but one that is hitting the FM technical practice especially hard, is hiring and retaining appropriately skilled workers. In former times, the US military services provided valuable training and experience in many of the technical skills required for FM practice. These well-trained technicians left military service and moved into commercial industries to design, plan, manage and service facilities since shortly after World War II through the late 1980s. But as military budgets are stretched, this training is no longer the stronghold that produced experienced workers for other industries; now the United States is left with a dwindling cadre of technical experts, and technical colleges and programs are not adequately filling current needs. Therefore, the successful FM practice in the near term will be the one that successfully locates, hires and retains technicians and technical managers. As it is said, "It's a dog-eat-dog world out there in facility-land," and only the astute and adaptable organisations will come out on top during this expected dearth of technically trained workers.

Whenever employees leave an organisation, knowledge as well as profits go with them. The time, energy and financial investment in their training and orientation to the organisation are lost; additionally, time, energy and cost then must be spent to bring a new employee on board and get him or her adequately trained. New employees typically enter the organisation at the bottom of the quality and productivity curves, which reduces the effectiveness and competitiveness of the practice. Skill shortages and training only raise costs, so employee retention, where possible, is a key competitive advantage.

Employee engagement, as described by Roper and Phillips (2007), suggests solving the dilemma of a minimized workforce through the development of a work culture and the hiring of employees who possess innovative and creative skills: those who take personal responsibility and have an authentic motivation for company success as well as their team's and personal success, including those who usually have an emotional bond with the company, its mission and its values, yet are also flexible enough to work with and adopt roles to fit clients' needs, as noted in this chapter. These engaged employees are motivated to provide superior customer service, and they know that this impacts the practice's bottom-line profitability and induces high levels of client satisfaction.

The younger generation, often referred to as Generation Y (or Gen-Y), coming into the workforce today has different motivations from previous generations of workers. After watching their parents compete for a few senior positions and suffer burnout and fatigue, Gen-Y desires a more balanced work and life scenario. They may be engaged, but they expect to work in various distributed ways, even as they serve client needs. They have grown up with, and are intimately familiar with, technological innovations and new ways of working to minimize their required time in the office, yet they are still alert to providing superior customer service in most cases. Not only do these young workers desire work life balance, but also they have shown to be especially interested in opportunities to develop and advance their careers through training, and they tend to remain longer with an employer who provides those benefits. A 2004 survey by Fairis (2004) of Gen-Y workers showed they would wait only an average of 10 months for an advancement opportunity to develop before concluding that advancement was blocked and they should look elsewhere for more rewarding career moves.

Succession plans can help to avoid the illusion of blocked opportunity, and although guarantees of advancement cannot be made in the contract world of FM practice, an investment in employee training to prepare them for future opportunities is one step toward increased engagement and retention. This is also a requirement if an organisation is to fill the voids of retiring and aging trained workers who are now or who soon will be leaving the workforce. All these workforce issues have a cost associated with them, but without the competitive advantage of skilled, engaged employees, the practice cannot maintain momentum and compete effectively in the current marketplace. Investments that balance the thin margin of profit with competitive advantage can keep FM practices valuable and essential to their clients.

Managing Scope Creep yet Maintaining a Customer Service Orientation

The reality of FM is that a careful balance between customer service and judiciary responsibility is an operational imperative. For the FM professional practice, the balance is made more difficult by the constant pressure from the customer to reduce costs yet maintain or even increase service levels and value. And nowhere does this balance become more precarious than when staying within the contract scope to avoid expansion of service without amendments to the contract.

Scope creep is the growth of a contract or project scope by inevitable changes that occur as time, expectations and reality change. This creep or expansion is a natural result of downward pressure for reduced costs and increased service and value by the customer. Such creep has to be identified and managed, as it requires additional payment rather than absorption. It must be managed in a firm, yet tactful, manner if the customer is to maintain the perception of quality and positive service from the provider.

Preventing any scope creep is almost impossible since rapid change in all types of business is the norm, but minimizing the amount and extent of the creep can usually be managed with strategic and thoughtful planning, and the customer will help to minimize it too as they realize that such additions do not come free.

The first step to minimising scope creep would be to initially set achievable contract perimeters for the practice. Overcommitting to the client to gain the contract can only backfire later when reality and tendencies for scope creep occur. This is a type of risk management. Realistic and achievable scope definition and discussion of these perimeters on a frequent basis with the client can help to minimize creep during the contract and provide a positive setting for dealing with inevitable changes. This aids in identifying creep as it occurs. When everyone understands the limits of the contract and this discussion is part of normal updates and reviews, the opportunity to address contract changes or amendments is much easier and well accepted by the client. This is the management of scope creep.

Negotiating contracts that provide a win–win for client and practice provider are the ideal environment in which to deal with scope creep. When a client expects honest interchange with a contractor, the atmosphere is much more conducive to discussing the limitations of the contract than an atmosphere in which the client tries to direct and manipulate the contractor into a win–lose position – with the client winning and the contractor losing, of course. The contract can even be structured to include language detailing how scope expansion will be handled and lay out specifics as to what and how much each party will handle in each situation.

Scope creep is usually a negative term, but in some instances, the more positive side of contract changes can benefit both the client and FM provider. Incentive clauses are becoming common with performance-based contracts. The client specifies expected outcomes rather than detailed specifications, and when the provider beats the outcomes in cost, value or satisfaction, there are remuneration rewards or other shared rewards that benefit the provider as well as the client. Clients who demand all savings are typically those who also do not understand performance-based contracts and do not benefit from good relationships with their providers (or employees, in most cases). These organisations are rarely as successful as their enlightened counterparts who tend to have a higher customer loyalty factor, making them more competitive and able to extend goodwill in all their interactions. Finding clients with these values is critical to expanding and growing an FM practice. Otherwise, the professional practice is constantly in 'defend and recover' mode with their clients as they manage change in the original scope and definitions of the contract for services.

Managing the scope change process, since it is inevitable, is required in almost all contracts. Some tips for success can be found by developing a formal change process, which includes having a simple document to request written changes; contract language, which includes authorisation levels for change approvals; a joint review between client and contractor to analyse the impact and costs of proposed changes; and, of course, the final approval and specification of changes, which must be signed by the appropriate-level officer as previously designated in the contract for such changes.

Another type of scope creep can essentially be called *client growth*. Once a practice demonstrates its expertise and fit with a client, it may have the opportunity to grow the business by either expanding the scope of service or expanding the breadth of facilities covered. Many organisations will limit its first contract with a professional practice as a risk assessment method to assure good fit and delivery of service. Once the FM practices is positively received, their ability to offer and gain expanded services can grow the contract, or they may add new contracts for additional services, enabling the growth of the professional practice.

Summary and Conclusions

The future for FM professional practice is not dissimilar to that of other businesses. Development of strong human resource management skills, along with ongoing technological updates, will be required for service professionals to maintain a profitable practice. Another key skill to aid business development and success of the practice in the future will be the ability to organize efficiently, develop networks for gaining client access, and stay abreast of the many business trends and changes that directly impact how clients expect to receive service, manage their bidding processes, and evaluate service in the FM arena. Staying in one-on-one contact with clients on a frequent basis can be a touchstone for superior service delivery.

As discussed in this chapter's opening comments, the temptation to be everything to everyone needs to be avoided. Sticking to areas of expertise or wisely affiliating with partners to expand services is the cautionary and more successful way to manage a professional practice. As stated by Herbert Bayard Swope, journalist and first winner of the Pulitzer Prize for Reporting, "I cannot give you the formula for success, but I can give you the formula for failure – which is: 'Try to please everybody'" (ThinkExist.com, 2013). It may be that professional firms try to increase their range of services and deliver these in a differentiated way as the economy grows. This possibility could be presented as a recommendation for practice, yet the market ultimately drives change such that academic research and recommendations form another influence, leaving managers to weigh up the whole picture.

References

Fairis, D. (2004). Internal labor markets and worker quits. *Industrial Relations.* 43(3), 573–594.

Franklin, P. (1997). Competitive advantage and core competencies. *Strategic Change.* 6, 371–375.

IFMA. (2009). What is FM? Available at: http://www.ifma.org/know-base/browse/what-is-fm- (accessed 2 July 2013).

Mockler, R.J. (1997). Multi-national strategic alliances: a manager's perspective. *Strategic Change*. 6, 391–405.

Porter, M. (1985). *Competitive Advantage*. New York: Free Press.

Prahalad, C.K., and Ramaswamy, V. (2004a). Co-creating experiences: the next practice in value creation. *Journal of Interactive Marketing*. 18(3), 5–14.

Prahalad, C.K., and Ramaswamy, V. (2004b). Co-creating unique value with customers. *Strategy & Leadership*, 32(3), 4–9.

Ring, P.S., and Van de Ven, A. (1994). Developmental processes of cooperative interorganizational relationships. *Academy of Management Review*, 19(1), 90–118.

Roper, K.O., and Phillips, D.R. (2007). Integrating self-managed work teams into project management, *Journal of Facilities Management*. 5(1), 22–36.

ThinkExist.com. (2009). [Herbert Bayard Swope quote]. Available at: http://thinkexist.com/quotation/i_cannot_give_you_the_formula_for_success-but_i/176509.html (accessed 2 July 2013).

Globalization of Facility Management

Kathy O. Roper

Georgia Institute of Technology, Atlanta, GA

The world is becoming smaller. As the facility management (FM) industry matures, we see that the practice is becoming widespread in developed as well as developing nations. However, the scale of expectations of responsibilities and skills varies from region to region and is primarily dependent on local maturity and knowledge. As a broad overview, it is realistic to say that FM is practiced in almost all parts of the world. The locations lacking FM consist of those without major urban areas or large-scale businesses. As has been found with the maturity of FM, the areas that are just adopting technology are also the ones beginning to learn and incorporate FM practice.

The practice of FM began formally in the United States and the United Kingdom in the late 1970s, as organizations began to realize that their built assets could provide key benefits if they were well managed and maintained. From there, the profession was quickly taken up in Europe and later in the larger cities of Asia. In more recent times, Australasia, South America and, to some extent, Eastern Europe have adopted the FM profession as one noteworthy of education and professionalization.

Since all of these regions have major differences in both the climate impacting facility operations as well as cultural, governmental and educational issues, we will address each area separately, comparing their history, their current state of the art and the prospects for FM as a formal profession.

International Facility Management, First Edition. Kathy O. Roper and Lisa J. Borello.
© 2014 John Wiley & Sons, Ltd. Published 2014 by John Wiley & Sons, Ltd.

Africa

Africa has adapted FM in a number of ways and at various levels around the continent; in the last decade, interest in and development of FM have increased rapidly in many countries. Nigeria, South Africa, and parts of Egypt have fully developed facility service providers and competitive smaller companies offering specific facility services. In Nigeria, the director general of the Lagos State Public Private Partnership (PPP), Mr. Ayo Gbeleyi, announced at a 2012 FM conference that the Lagos government has instituted various regulatory procedures to encourage FM and investors. Additionally, the government has provided the Public Works Bureau (PWC) in Nigeria, charged with infrastructure maintenance in the state, with an enabling environment for prospective investors through relevant legislation regarding the built environment (Ogunyooye, 2012).

Countries have also adopted legislation related to sustainable building and operations. South Africa has created the Green Building Council SA in Cape Town and follows the Green Star SA rating tool. Similar to other Green Star systems modeled after the Australian Green Star rating system, the South African version has not been required in major cities across the country, but it is referenced in the major cities' own development guides. Similar to the programs of many countries around the world, the voluntary nature of most sustainability programs means that until consumers and the general public fully comprehend sustainability in the built environment, there will be minimal compliance with these guides. However, as African countries rapidly gain a maintenance culture, skilled personnel, technologies and built infrastructures, they have the opportunity to "leap frog" older technologies and start with the newest versions, sometimes at lower costs than more developed countries paid for their initial investments. This dynamic environment gives emerging economies a great advantage if they are able to leverage it with government backing and financial support. While aging infrastructure in Europe and North America requires great costs when older assets are replaced, emerging economies across Africa can adopt the latest technologies as they build their infrastructure. FM professionals familiar with life-cycle costing see the promise across Africa as towns grow and develop into cities across the continent. As a result, professionalization of the built environment has great opportunity throughout Africa.

The education systems in Egypt, South Africa and Nigeria have begun to explore FM course work in their construction, real estate and management faculties. However, most training is provided currently by specialized vendors, such as ALPHAMEAD Facilities and Management Services Limited, WSP FMC Nigeria Limited and Domme Facilities Management Limited, which provide facility services (A. Mosuro, personal communication, January 20, 2013), or the larger professional associations focused on FM, such as the International Facility Management Association (IFMA), the European Facility Management Network (EuroFM) or the Royal Institute of Chartered Surveyors (RICS). South Africa is leading the way in adoption and formal education in FM, with many multinational corporations, universities and professional associations focused on aspects of FM. Many students from across the continent travel to South Africa to gain this expertise, which is then dispersed back across Africa.

For example, Nigeria has 40 federal universities, 38 state universities, 50 private universities, 21 federal polytechnics, 38 state polytechnics, 16 private polytechnics, 21 federal colleges of education, 46 state colleges of education and 33 private colleges of education, all of which are recognized higher institutions of learning. Of these, only Ahmadu Bello University (a federal university) Zaria, which currently runs first- and second-degree programs in FM; the University of Lagos, which currently offers a Diploma and Master's Program on FM; and the Obafemi Awolowo University, also a federal university, are the only three institutions shaping the future of FM practice in Nigeria (A. Mosuro, personal communication, January 28, 2013).

FM practice is relatively new in Nigeria because the profession was once dominated by real estate managers, rather than professional facility managers. Coupled with the incorporation of the IFMA Nigeria chapter in 1997, more FM professionals and firms, like ALPHAMEAD Facilities and Management Services Limited, WSP FMC Nigeria Limited and Domme Facilities Management Limited, have dominated the scene and demonstrated the true professionalism expected of a young and vibrant but growing profession. Ever since FM practice started to assume and dominate the leadership role of management in Nigeria, a number of real estate firms, such as Filmo Realty Limited and Charles Adebiyi and Company, to mention a few, have added FM services to their line of work.

Arising primarily from the growth of multinational organizations in Africa, the recognition of FM as a need and as a profession is growing. As more assets are developed and as more focus on life-cycle needs is shared as best practice among organizations, the FM component grows stronger. However, many organizations are choosing to focus on core competencies, and the primary growth in FM across Africa is seen in facility service companies that provide FM services to organizations as a core function. Just within Nigeria, FM practice is gaining prominence, and today the IFMA Nigeria chapter has over 700 individual and 100 corporate registered members (IFMA Nigeria President Mr. Tony Ezeaku, personal communication, January 27, 2013). This is perhaps as it should be, so that facility professionals focus on the facility and organizations focus on their products and/or services, hiring facility service organizations to develop, maintain and operate their buildings.

Expected growth is anticipated in areas that are rapidly growing. As facilities are added for commerce, residences and services such as retail, healthcare, airports or cultural facilities, there is broad opportunity for growth, but it will be slow until the profession is broadly understood in Africa.

Asia

As the largest and dominant nation in Asia, China has led efforts to develop and advance the FM profession over the last decade, with a focus on "property" as the preferred terminology (Gilleard, 2005). Most of this development comes from Hong Kong, with additional growth in Taiwan; however, mainland China is beginning the development of property and FM job classifications that enable focused growth and recognition of the profession. With an estimated 1.3 billion residents (World Bank, 2013), China has tremendous opportunity for improved management of properties and facilities among its many recently built high-rise buildings and those currently under construction across the country. As these buildings are completed and occupied, there has been minimal focus on their ongoing upkeep; instead, the local focus is typically around newer and newer construction across the country.

With an influx of multinational organizations, especially commercial and retail operations like hotels and shopping malls, entering China, the expectation for life-cycle maintenance planning and operations is likewise moving into China. Since government recognition and certification of all job positions are required within China, this aspect of FM develop is unique. Most FM throughout the world evolved from technical services, to increasing management responsibility, to maturity as a profession with organizational value added through ever-expanding expertise across the broad spectrum of facility responsibilities. However, China's regulatory environment places the responsibility for the professional development of FM upfront, so that recognition of facility services is needed before citizens are trained and enter the profession. This leaves a huge gap in the current needs of mainland China for trained facility operators and managers.

Currently, one positive move for FM is the No. 18 Decree of the Ministry of Labour and Social Security, which was enacted in 2007 when IFMA's credentials, Facility Management Professional (FMP) and Certified Facility Manager (CFM), received official permission to be implemented in the People's Republic of China (PRC). It must be understood that permission to launch the IFMA credentials did not guarantee market success in China, since the maturity level and industry recognition of FM in China are still very low, and have no support from industry or the PRC government at this time. There is no incentive for the Chinese people to learn about FM since workers there normally follow the government's direction (O. Chan, personal communication, January 28, 2013).

In addition, not only are foreign vocational qualifications required to have permission before being launched in China, but also another critical issue relates to employment eligibility in China. The PRC Ministry of Human Resources and Social Security has an employment system whereby official lists of occupations that demand certain training are approved, thus giving graduates recognized skills or qualifications that entail specified market pay and benefits. The qualification, known as "上崗證" (which is equivalent to a "licensed work permit"), applies to many different skills and professions. In the past, FM was not recognized by the PRC government as a skill that warrants the issue of licensed work permit.

Despite the approval of IFMA credentials granted in China, the response for licensed work permission has been close to zero. Collaboration between the Macao government and Guangdong (GD) provincial government since December 2011 has garnered approval for FM training (at three levels) under the PRC National Vocational Qualification (NVQ), titled a "one exam three certificates" scheme, which now has become one of the recognized occupations in the GD province. With government official recognition of FM at three basic levels, it is expected that there will be much more interest for people to learn and wish to be qualified under this training scheme (O. Chan, personal communication, January 28, 2013).

One recurring issue in China is concern for quality in products as well as services. One study by Kull and Wacker (2010) found that, contrary to expectations, many cultural dimensions did not have significant impacts on quality management processes, but, as expected, China had the least effective use of quality management. As a service industry, FM is heavily dependent on strong customer service delivery and quality imperatives. If Chinese FM is to flourish, this issue needs to be addressed to bring China into parity with other FM service delivery cultures around the world.

India is another blossoming region for FM. The growth required to keep up with population, coupled with the advances in education, income and lifestyle in the major cities of India, require that attention is paid to usability, operability and maintainability issues at the outset of creation of the many buildings and complexes currently being built across India. In the past, buildings were built with little consideration of how they would be operated and maintained. As developers realize the need to maximize their investments, many are looking for basic FM services.

This need for training in basic facility services is critical across India. While visiting New Delhi and Bangalore in early 2012, the author found that every developer, real estate firm and multinational service provider was seeking basic training in order to hire qualified workers to maintain and operate their buildings, affirming that FM is at the basic operational level throughout India. Many of the large firms and universities are recognizing this need and beginning to offer training. However, the need is far outstripping the current training that is available.

With little governmental involvement and more multilingual speakers in India than in other Asian countries, the opportunity for advancement of FM there is great. With high potential growth in India, for example more than 500 airports expected to be built there over the next 10 years (B. Agarwal, personal communication, February 10, 2012), there is a need to quickly train workers to maximize the life of these facilities and to ensure that these assets maintain their value for the owners. The growth of FM could be substantial in India, and most FM professional associations are working with facility owners and facility services providers to help advance the profession as the population desires.

The prestigious India Institute of Technology in New Delhi currently offers a master's degree in real estate and offers courses in FM. They have also begun to develop continuing education courses to bring professional training to the region and further develop facility education. Other universities may be following their success and launching their own programs, which could benefit greatly from the expansion of FM as it becomes more widely recognized.

Indonesia is another region of Asia with cities that have become fairly sophisticated in the built environment. Large multinational companies and the education system in Indonesia have successfully provided a growing number of environmentally responsible complex facilities, primarily in the large cities of Jakarta, Singapore, Surabaya, Bandung and Bekasi. Several universities across Indonesia are providing degrees in FM or related fields, and the government agencies associated with the built environment are all eager to provide FM training and development within Indonesia. Two universities in Singapore have gained accreditation from the IFMA Foundation: SIM University, School of Science and Technology, offers a Bachelor Program in Facilities and Events Management; and Temasek Polytechnic offers a Diploma Program (3 years) in Integrated Facility Management (IFMA Foundation, 2013).

Malaysia is another Asian island and peninsular country that has a rapidly developing FM profession, especially in the capital of Kuala Lumpur and in Johor Bahru. These large cities host many international organizations, and the uptake of FM there has been steadily increasing over the last decade. With neighboring Indonesia offering university-level education, most training in Malaysia at this time is proprietary to facility service organizations. So additional opportunities abound for growth of FM in the smaller Asian countries, as well as the larger nations.

Australasia

The Australasian region includes Australia, New Zealand, New Guinea and neighboring islands in the Pacific Ocean (Wikipedia, 2013). It is a diverse region, and the continent of Australia and neighboring New Zealand have had a strong background with FM since the mid-1980s. The Facility

Management Association of Australia (FMA) was chartered in 1989 and has branches across Australia in the Australian Capital Territory, New South Wales, Queensland, South Australia, Victoria and Western Australia. With major cities in these areas, there are also university degrees and certificates in FM in all regions.

Australian FM has been internationally connected with FM in the United Kingdom, the United States and other Asian locations since its inception, and it has benefitted from shared information and knowledge. International FM conferences for researchers and practitioners are well attended by Australians, demonstrating their interest and maturity in FM development. FM in Australia is also closely linked to the environmental issues of the built environment through the Green Building Council of Australia and the Green Star Performance rating tool, especially the Existing Building Operation sector. Australia is seen as the mature leader in the region regarding FM.

New Zealand has been newer in adopting FM as a unique and valuable profession. With fewer large cities and an agricultural base throughout much of the two islands comprising New Zealand, the professional association, Facilities Management Association of New Zealand (FMANZ), was launched in 2010 and held its first conference in 2012. Rapid development is anticipated, although large growth is not possible in this limited country. Participating in the international FM arena is helping FMANZ and its members to quickly come to high maturity levels by sharing knowledge from other regions. It is noteworthy that FM in New Zealand is quickly becoming an advocate for the promotion of public health in buildings and protection of the fragile New Zealand environment.

The neighboring islands of the Pacific do not generally have a mature infrastructure and research or education about the built environment and FM. Without large cities to command attention in this area, most of the focus around the islands is on hospitality and resort management, in addition to normal local governmental facilities and needs. FM is practiced but not in large numbers or with large facilities on most islands.

Europe

The practice of FM in Central Europe dates to the late 1970s and early 1980s. As described in its history on the EuroFM website, the 1985 development of the first association in Europe quickly led to diverse development across the multicultural, lingual, economic and governmental areas of Europe. In 1993, EuroFM was officially registered, and in 2002 development of the standard European definition of FM was launched with "EN15221-1: 2006 Facility Management – Part 1: Terms and Definitions," with final adoption by the EU government in 2006 (EuroFM, 2013).

One of the hallmarks of FM in Europe has been the acceptance of diversity throughout the 27 EU countries. In some areas, FM relates primarily to real estate and workplace considerations, with other areas focusing on services (from either maintenance or food services backgrounds) as dominant. Another focus has been the development of FM as a hospitality service, bringing in the customer service focus as a major determinant of metrics. The work accomplished to pass the EN15221-1 definition across Europe was a major milestone in bringing together the diverse countries of Europe to enable work across borders and expand the recognition of FM overall.

Eastern Europe came into the European Union later, and, therefore, these countries also have taken up FM more recently. However, these countries have quickly entered FM, especially the facility services sector. As a single region, Eastern and Western Europe are moving toward building a strong impact for FM across Europe. As stated in the EuroFM website,

> At the start of 2011 the EuroFM association represented 100 organisations working in the € 650 billion large European FM sector. Our sector is the largest European Business Services market, the second largest European sector (5–8% of GDP) and the largest FM market in the world. (EuroFM, 2013)

Universities across Europe have embraced FM education, and numerous certificate, baccalaureate and graduate programs exist in almost every European country. Diversity has enabled some countries to specialize in specific areas of FM; for example, Dutch universities have nine degree-granting programs in FM and hospitality services. The United Kingdom has long used its research centres to focus on issues to advance FM and workplace concerns.

Many of the individual European countries have specific associations for FM. In the United Kingdom, the British Institute of Facilities Management (BIFM), Facility Management Netherlands (FMN), the Romanian Facility Management Association (RFMA) and many others exist and work in coordination with EuroFM to share knowledge and information. The International Facility Management Association also has several chapters in countries like Austria, Spain, Switzerland and Sweden. The Nordic countries of Denmark, Finland, Iceland, Norway and Sweden also participate in the NordicFM organization, which started in 2003. With a fairly mature FM industry across Europe, working with other countries and associations and sharing knowledge have helped to continue the advancement of FM throughout the region. As these countries deal with aging infrastructure, increasing diversity and new economic models for cross-border exchange, there will be new learning required and continued advancement of the profession.

Middle East

The development of formal FM has been recent in the Gulf Cooperation Council (GCC) states, which include Bahrain, Kuwait, Oman, Qatar, Saudi Arabia and United Arab Emirates. Probably emerging from the many multinational oil companies in the region, the management of large facilities was originally handled independently by owners. With worldwide recognition and growth of facility service provision in the region, the Middle East Facility Management Association (MEFMA) was formed from the real estate sector to unite and support FM professionals in the region.

With a strong focus on heavy industrial facilities, such as the oil industry, new attention on the huge commercial office spaces in the Middle East is expanding the understanding and need for FM professionals in this region. A background in engineering and real estate forms the dominate competencies of facility managers in the region, but growth into other competencies is booming business in the Middle East. Training by MEFMA and other organizations like BIFM, IFMA and independent training companies has helped to bring maturity rapidly to the region. The training is available across the GCC states and appears to be growing as the region continues to build more and more commercial structures. As with other emerging regions, the FM skill set of most workers is at the basic level; however, numerous multinational facility service companies have entered the market yet struggle to hire qualified workers. This is the reason for the large training opportunities in the region.

With strong economies through the Middle East, the growth of buildings and large facilities is expected to continue to grow in upcoming decades. This will provide for continued expansion of FM in the region and necessitate ongoing training for skilled workers.

to broader value within organizations is expected. With a strong history of outsourcing as the main delivery method for FM, this model is not expected to change over time.

North America

As one of the locations launching FM in the late 1970s, North America, primarily the United States and Canada, has a mature and broad definition and acceptance of FM professionals in its governments and businesses. Founded in 1979 in Michigan, the National Facility Management Association expanded into Canada in 1980 and renamed itself the International Facility Management Association, recognizing the growth possibilities for FM. This was the first professional association for facility managers, many of whom were just learning their new titles. As former building engineers, administrative services directors or people with similar titles, these facility managers focused on management of the facility as an outcome of the proliferation of personal computers and open-landscape office design, giving rise to the need for more strategic and frequent management of spaces for office workers.

In 1980, the first FM formal education program was launched in the United States, and Canada followed closely behind (Cornell University, 2013). Since that time, the need for higher education has grown, and there are currently about 25 programs teaching various levels of facility management education, from associate to bachelor and even graduate degrees in the field.

Current practice of FM is spearheaded by leading specialist companies providing facility services, as well as by many large corporations and the US and Canadian governments, who manage large portfolios of spaces. Many of these organizations conduct regular benchmarking and best practice comparisons, either on their own or via consultants, so that the maturity level is generally very high. As these practices filter down, the general business climate is very accepting of FM and the value it brings to a mid- to large-sized organization. While titles of occupations in the industry still vary widely, the sharing of information in trade publications and through professional associations related to facility management has standardized and elevated the profession. Some organizations, primarily multinationals or governments, have begun to elevate the senior oversight position to that of Chief Facility Management Executive (CFMO) or another c-suite title. As the professionalization continues in more and more organizations, the value of strategically planning and managing facilities is expected to expand.

Technology and the rapid advance of integration for built environment technologies in the last half-decade have also matured and changed the FM landscape. More automation of building components, the ability to integrate systems providing additional intelligence and reporting as well as the advance of building information modeling (BIM) throughout all phases of planning, constructing and operating buildings have led to new requirements and skill levels for facility professionals. No longer is technology the only skill needed, but advanced leadership, communication and business knowledge require that those entering the facility field today have a broad skill set or plan to learn one quickly.

Another expanding concept in North America is the use of outsourced specialists for many or most facility service functions. These specialists have merged and acquired additional expertise, and some now offer fully integrated facility services. For many organizations, the use of these specialists is becoming more routine, leaving senior FM executives to manage contracts and provide strategic oversight of functions related to managing the workplace, built environment and related services.

Growth for FM in North America is difficult to predict accurately, but with an aging population of experienced FMs, the expectation is that more and more new FMs will be needed as those skilled professionals eventually retire and leave the workforce. However, timing for this exit has been difficult to estimate accurately, due to financial issues forcing many employees to remain longer in the workforce than originally anticipated, or perhaps as societal norms change and individuals remain active workers for longer periods. This delay has aided the ability of North American education systems to expand the formalized offerings in FM and related fields.

South and Central America

The history of FM in Central and South America is new and fairly limited when compared to other areas of the world. A tradition of engineering and real estate is well developed in many South American nations, but the ties to FM have been slow to develop there. Perhaps Brazil is the most advanced nation in FM, and other rapidly advancing economies in Argentina, Columbia, Mexico and some of the Caribbean nations are following. Like many of the emerging areas mentioned in this book, this part of the world has been fairly isolated from many business developments until the recent past. As economies stabilize and become more active in international commerce, governments and large multinational organizations are becoming active in developing and managing this region's built environment.

Today the only known FM formal education program throughout the region is the University of São Paulo's real estate and FM program. Other real estate programs are available, but they focus on development and acquisition issues. Building operations are still focused in the individual engineering programs and, in some cases, are not developed fully for education beyond the design and construction stages of the building. As typically developed in other markets, the initial phases of built environment design and construction lead the educational offerings in Central and South America. It is anticipated that normal development coupled with the entry of multinational organizations into the area will expedite the development and maturity of FM. Some of the facility services are already beginning to develop in the region.

Brazil's professional association, Associação Brasileira de Facilities (ABRAFAC), was founded in 2004 and now has approximately 400 members across Brazil (ABRAFAC, 2013). This group brings together those with an interest in FM and provides them with resources, networking and connectivity to the broader worldwide network of facility professionals. Many facility service companies and multinational organizations participate in ABRAFAC, which hosts events and meetings in the larger Brazilian cities.

Interest in FM by global providers, as well as local real estate, construction and entrepreneurial organizations with diverse backgrounds, is fueling rapid development. A primary issue for development will be the ability of service providers to establish profitable clientele in specific markets in the larger cities across the region. Stabilization of financial exchange, inflation and investment rates will dictate the rate of acceptance, as will the expansion of global organizations into the region. Expected growth may be slow in the immediate future, but potential is building and expected to remain positive in the future.

Summary and Conclusions

The understanding of FM is spreading rapidly.

Spurred on by sustainability initiatives and an understanding that the built environment is a valuable asset to be planned for, preserved and well maintained, businesses are finally recognizing the value and importance of the broad FM profession. As emerging economies learn about current practices in more developed areas, they are "leap frogging" to gain rapid competitive advantages since they are unencumbered with a large, obsoleting infrastructure.

The future is bright for the industry in general. As presented in the separate region sections of this chapter, there are areas with large growth potential, including the need for basic training in the emerging economies. The more developed nations are generally providing mature FM, and they may see growth in only technological developments and retrofits of existing buildings, with limited expansion of populations and new construction. With huge growth potential in developing nations, a growing educational base and increasing recognition with financial sectors, opportunities for FM employment and skill levels continue to rise worldwide.

References

Associação Brasileira de Facilities (ABRAFAC). (2013). [Home page]. Available at: http://www.abrafac.org.br (accessed 10 January 2013).
Cornell University. (2013). BS Facilities Planning and Management. Available at: http://www.human.cornell.edu/dea/academics/undergraduate/fpm/index.cfm (accessed 12 December 2012).
European Facility Management Network. (EuroFM). (2013). What is FM? Available at: http://eurofm.org/about-us/what-is-fm/ (accessed 3 January 2013).
Gilleard, J. (2005). Facility management in China: an emerging market. Available at: www.ifma.org.hk/download/JohnGilleard.pdf (accessed 20 January 2013).
IFMA Foundation. (2013). Accredited degree program. Available at: http://www.ifmafoundation.org/accredited-degree/ (accessed 20 December 2012).
Kull, T.J., and Wacker, J. (2010). Quality management effectiveness in Asia: the influence of culture. *Journal of Operations Management.* 28 (3), 223–239.

Ogunyooye, O. (2012). Real estate value: facility managers harp on global best practice. Available at: http://connectnigeria.com/articles/2012/07/04/real-estate-value-facility-managers-harp-on-global-best-practice/ (accessed 29 December 2012).

Wikipedia. (2013). Australasia. Available at: http://en.wikipedia.org/wiki/Australasia (accessed 2 February 2013).

World Bank. (2013). China. Available at: http://www.worldbank.org/en/country/china (accessed 28 December 2012).

Sustainability and Carbon Reporting

Chris Hodges

Facility Engineering Associates and George Mason University, Fairfax, VA

Financial results were once regarded as the only true measure of success in business. Since the last one-third of the twentieth century, however, our commitment to society and to the environment has gained significant ground in businesses, governments, and nongovernmental organizations around the world. A new way to measure success is to provide non-financial metrics side by side with traditional financial measures. These nonfinancial indicators are used to demonstrate corporate social responsibility (CSR), a measure of commitment to sustainability. Organizational leaders have realized that they can use their commitment to sustainability as a means of enhancing their attractiveness to stakeholders and improving the quality of life for their constituents. Sustainability initiatives that enhance quality of life, conserve resources, and protect the environment have become the language of CSR for organizations of all types.

The purpose of this chapter is to evaluate the role of the facility manager in sustainability and carbon reporting and focus on those processes and standards that govern facility-related issues. The facility manager is typically not in the role of making organizational decisions related to overall operations; however, in the area of sustainability, the facility management professional can play an important consulting role by persuasively demonstrating the value of sustainability efforts and the impact they provide to the overall organization. Several tools are available to help the facility professional demonstrate the value of implementing sustainability measures, including the Global Reporting Initiative (GRI), which is quickly becoming the most widespread tool used throughout the world. This chapter also discusses the role that facility managers can play in measuring greenhouse gas emissions,

International Facility Management, First Edition. Kathy O. Roper and Lisa J. Borello.
© 2014 John Wiley & Sons, Ltd. Published 2014 by John Wiley & Sons, Ltd.

as well as their impact on the workplace and life-cycle management. These and other new ways of drawing attention to environmental and social issues in business are becoming a critical part of the field of facility management.

Drivers of Sustainability

The environmental impacts of our organizational actions became important decades ago, when industry learned that there were significant risks in using up valuable resources, despoiling nature, and exposing workers and civil society to harm. Societal concerns were soon to follow when we learned of unacceptable labor practices and organizations taking advantage of populations for economic gain. There is little doubt that environmentally harmful practices and exploitation of people around the world for economic gain have occurred for centuries. However, it has been only over the last few decades that we have been able to see the consequences of those actions. The most common definition of sustainability comes from the 1987 UN Brundtland Commission report titled *Our Common Future* (United Nations, 1987). Although the Commission's focus was from the broad perspective of international development, the concept that we need to preserve our resources for future generations has become the baseline definition of sustainability in all industries worldwide.

Another significant development in the language of sustainability was the articulation of the triple bottom line. The triple bottom line is the framework that describes an organization's commitment to the environment and to society, as well as its traditional and well-understood commitment to the economic impact of its actions. While large corporations have always existed for the financial benefit of their stakeholders, the triple bottom line is able to add two important aspects that stakeholders tend to value – the effect of the organization's actions on the environment, and its effect on society. CSR is a public display of an organization's commitment to the triple bottom line.

With the Internet, cell phones with cameras, 24-hour news, and social media, harms to people and to the environment are more apparent. Communication is instantaneous, and exposure is unavoidable. In today's world, it is easy to see where things are produced, who produced them, and the conditions under which they were produced. Even in the service industry, we recognize that the person on the other end of the customer service phone line may be thousands of miles away and that the food we just ordered in our favorite local restaurant may have come from just as far.

As information becomes more readily available around the globe, organizations are experiencing a visibility that they have never dealt with before. Actions are no longer judged by the output of the marketing department; rather, they are judged by an organization's demonstration of commitment to the triple bottom line and by the magnitude and speed of its reactions to negative social and environmental events. Reporting of those commitments and resulting actions have become a source of competitive advantage in business, and transparency in reporting has become much more important. Sustainability reporting is becoming just as important as financial accounting to many stakeholders. CEOs and corporate boards have also seized the opportunity to show their commitment to the triple bottom line as a means of demonstrating competence and inspiring the confidence of their stakeholders.

Sustainability Reporting

Financial reporting has always been important for organizations that want to attract buyers, investors, and followers. The importance of sustainability reporting, however, has grown with globalization and as stakeholders demand better corporate citizenship.

There is an old adage that you cannot manage what you cannot measure, and that you cannot change what you cannot manage. While the financial world has had decades to bring structure and consistency to financial reporting, sustainability reporting to the triple bottom line is still in its adolescent stage and will most likely require several more years to mature to the level of consistency of financial reporting. Although there are many reporting frameworks and methodologies for environmental and social issues, few have made as much progress as the Global Reporting Initiative (GRI; www.globalreporting.org). The GRI was created by the US non-profit organization Coalition for Environmentally Responsible Economies (CERES). The GRI is a nonprofit organization consisting of thousands of stakeholders that are interested in making sustainability reporting a standard practice by providing guidance and support to all types of organizations. Since the early 1990s, the GRI has promoted one of the world's leading platforms for corporate and organizational sustainability reporting. The purpose of the framework is to allow investors and other stakeholders a view into the environmental and social commitments of organizations.

As of 2012, the GRI reporting framework was in its third iteration, G3.1, and the G4 framework is due to be launched in 2013. (Global Reporting Initiative, 2011). The framework consists of a set of standard disclosures and performance indicators that fit into one of six key areas that map to the triple bottom line. The six categories are listed in Table 5.1.

The categories each have a number of organizational characteristics and behaviors that are monitored in order to provide a complete picture of organizational commitment to the triple bottom line. Each aspect has a corresponding set of indicators (measures) that are either required (core) or optional (additional).

Table 5.1 The triple bottom line, and GRI reporting categories, aspects, and indicators

	Triple bottom line		
Environmental	Social		Economic
	Global Reporting Initiative G3.1 framework		
Category	Number of aspects	Examples of aspects	Number of indicators	Examples of indicators
Society	5	Community commitment, corruption practices, and compliance issues	8	Percentage of operations with community engagement; monetary value of significant fines
Human rights	9	Nondiscrimination, freedom of association, no child labor or forced labor	11	Total number of incidents of discrimination; percentage of operations subject to human rights review
Labor practices and decent work	6	Labor–management relations, occupational health and safety, training, and education	14	Percentage of employees covered by collective bargaining; average hours of training
Product responsibility	5	Customer health and safety, product labeling, marketing communications, and compliance	9	Programs for adherence to laws, standards, and voluntary codes; monetary value of significant fines
Environmental	9	Materials, energy, water, emissions, effluents and waste, products and services, and transport	30	GHG by weight, water withdrawn by source; energy consumption by primary source (direct and indirect)
Economic	3	Economic performance, market presence, and indirect economic impacts	9	Direct economic value generated and distributed, procedures for local hiring; development and impact of infrastructure investments

Standard disclosure requirements include an organization's disclosure on management approach (DMA) which includes the following:

- Goals and performance
- Policy
- Organizational responsibility
- Training and awareness
- Monitoring and follow-up
- Additional contextual information.

Additional indicators are provided in sector supplements. Sector supplements are specific to industries, such as mining and metals, construction and real estate, airport operators, and electric utilities.

The GRI reporting structure is built around an application level of A through C, with a plus (+) rating for each (i.e. A+, B+, and C+), for a total of six reporting levels, with A+being the most comprehensive and inclusive of the most aspects and indicators. Each reporting level requires some level of disclosure of the DMA, and a minimum number of performance indicators and sector supplement indicators.

For example, the minimum GRI report level is a C, and it requires that the organization report on a number of organizational profile disclosures (28 elements) and a minimum of 10 performance indicators, including at least one from each of the following: economic, social, and environmental. There are no management approach disclosures for a level-C report. A report becomes a "GRI report" when the organization declares an Application Level (A, B, or C). The Application Level is self-declared. Third-party and GRI "assured" reports can lead to the plus (+) designation.

The GRI framework relies on the concept of materiality. Materiality has its roots in financial reporting and is an indicator of the level of importance the aspect holds to the organization and its stakeholders. One of the advantages of using the GRI framework is that it requires a rigorous self-evaluation of the materiality of organizational characteristics as they relate to a wide range of stakeholders, not just the senior management of the organization itself. Use of the framework also requires an organization to set boundaries that define parts of the organization, its supply chain, and affiliated divisions and entities so that they can clearly define their level of control and influence.

The GRI is also closely integrated with the United Nations Global Compact (UNGC; www.unglobalcompact.org), and carbon measurement and assessment tools such as the Carbon Disclosure Project (CDP; www.cdproject.net). The UNGC is an international initiative that requires commitment to 10 principles surrounding the concepts of human rights, labor, environment, and anticorruption. The GRI provides a common framework to allow an organization to report on performance and compliance with the 10 principles of the UNGC. The UNGC principles can be tied to aspects and indicators of the GRI protocol.

The CDP was launched in 2000 and consists of an independent global system for reporting of greenhouse gas emissions, water usage, and assessment of climate change risk and opportunity. The mission of the CDP is to "accelerate solutions to climate change" by the sharing of relevant information in making investment, policy, and business decisions (Carbon Disclosure Project, 2012). The CDP manages programs that gather information on climate change:

- Investor CDP – gathering of carbon information for institutional investors
- CDP supply chain – gathering of carbon information on behalf of customers
- CDP water disclosure – gathering of water information on behalf of institutional investors
- CDP Cities – gathering of carbon information from cities.

Programs such as the CDP and the Greenhouse Gas Protocol Initiative of the World Resources Institute (www.wri.org) provide a number of tools, calculators, and protocols for the evaluation and quantification of important natural resources, like water and the emission of greenhouse gases. The World Business Council for Sustainable Development (WBCSD; www.wbcsd.org) has a Global Water Tool that is useful for facility managers in tracking water consumption. The Global Water Tool program integrates the measurement results for water use with the GRI water metrics. Choosing the right tool can be challenging and is typically industry specific. For buildings, facility managers need to choose specific analysis and measurement programs that are easily adapted to their consumption and use of major utilities such as electricity and natural gas, and their related emissions.

Many organizations have also developed performance and quality management systems to manage their commitment to CSR and the triple bottom line (Epstein, 2008). The International Organization for Standardization (ISO; www.iso.org) has created a set of voluntary standards for environmental performance. The ISO 14000 series of standards provide a framework for sustainability issues and the communication of organizational commitment to stakeholders.

The ISO 14064 series for environmental management provides guidance for the quantification and reporting of greenhouse gas emissions. This three-part series provides guidelines for developing and managing a reporting system at an organizational level, evaluating greenhouse gas emissions for projects, and engaging in processes for validation of inventories. ISO standards 14065 and 14066 deal with competency requirements for verification bodies. ISO 50001 provides guidance for developing energy management policies, objectives, and targets. It is important to note that the ISO standards help provide a structured approach for creating an energy management (ISO 50001) and environ-mental management (ISO 14000) system. ISO standards promote processes for developing and maintaining programs, promote continuous improvement, and leave the goals and targets for the organization to set.

Different countries have developed unique approaches to the challenges of environmental stewardship, climate change, resource management, and waste disposal. These approaches have led to an integration of sustainable initiatives into business practices and public life with a mixture of voluntary and mandatory requirements. New programs are being developed every day, and the pressure for mandatory disclosure of sustainable practices is growing.

Sustainability and the Facility Manager

The facility manager is usually not at the forefront of the organization's environmental or sustainability movement. The drivers of sustainability and CSR often exist at levels within an organization well above the day-to-day management of buildings and the workplace.

A gap exists between most organizations' philosophy toward the triple bottom line and how they manage their physical assets – their facilities.

Esty and Winston, in their book *Green to Gold*, explore the role of greenhouse gas emissions in explaining the concept of life-cycle management (Esty and Winston, 2006). Their example of looking at three different industries – auto manufacturing, a service business with an office environment, and a consumer goods company – illustrates where the largest portion of their carbon footprint lies. Figure 5.1 is

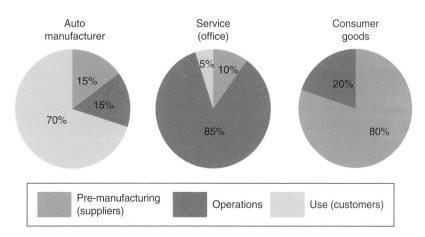

Figure 5.1   Life-cycle greenhouse gas emission (adapted from Esty and Winston, 2006).

an illustration of where most of the carbon emissions from each of these businesses occurs – during pre-manufacturing (from suppliers), during operations, or during use of the product or service. In the auto industry, most of the carbon emissions come from the use of the product. In the service business, the buildings that house the workforce produce most of the emissions. In the case of the consumer goods company, the majority of carbon emissions occur during pre-manufacturing, or in the supply chain.

Facility managers play different roles in sustainability reporting depending on which industry they represent. This type of organizational "emissions profile" can serve as an indicator of the level of involvement of a facility manager in an organization's overall sustainability-reporting efforts.

As illustrated by the life-cycle emissions profile of the service business in Figure 5.1, building operations account for significant portions of greenhouse gas emission, as well as energy use and contributions to the waste stream. However significant and unique this opportunity to manage energy input and waste output, there may be even greater value in the facility manager's influence over the productivity, health, and safety of the workforce through effective management of the workplace.

There are three primary areas of "influence" that the facility manager has on the sustainable operations of a facility. The first and most obvious is in the management of the building and the systems that consume resources, such as energy, water, and materials. The second area of major influence is in the management of the workplace. This area includes effective space management, building access (including commuting and parking), and management of occupant services. The third and often ignored area of influence is the facility manager's role in choosing and implementing repairs, restoration, upgrades, and additions with systems and materials that have a long service life.

A long service life with the appropriate durable materials is in itself a sustainable practice. These three areas of influence are shown in Figure 5.2.

The facility manager's role in the first area of influence (building management) will consist primarily of measurement, monitoring, and finding effective ways to reduce consumption. In workplace management, health, safety, productivity, and convenience of the workplace will define the facility manager's role in sustainable operations. Efficient use of space and effective workplace environments for promoting health and productivity are sustainable practices. The use of life-cycle costing, total cost of ownership, and durability of materials and systems forms the basis of the third area of influence for the facility manager. From inception to design and construction, operating and maintaining, capital renewal, and disposal, the facility manager is involved in the process for

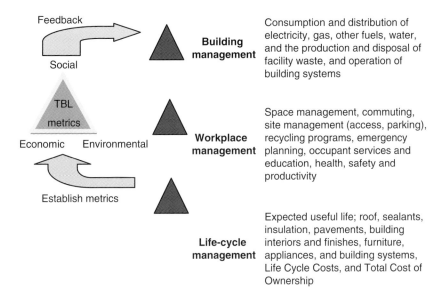

Feedback

Social

Building management

Consumption and distribution of electricity, gas, other fuels, water, and the production and disposal of facility waste, and operation of building systems

TBL metrics

Economic   Environmental

Establish metrics

Workplace management

Space management, commuting, site management (access, parking), recycling programs, emergency planning, occupant services and education, health, safety and productivity

Life-cycle management

Expected useful life; roof, sealants, insulation, pavements, building interiors and finishes, furniture, appliances, and building systems, Life Cycle Costs, and Total Cost of Ownership

Figure 5.2 Three "areas of influence" for the facility manager in managing sustainable facilities (adapted from National Science and Technology Council, Committee on Technology, 2008).

the entire life cycle of the facility. The facility manager plays a role in design and renovation teams in choosing efficient and long-lived systems that are easily accessible and maintainable, and then manages the remainder of the life cycle.

Sustainability Reporting

Although it is not likely that the facility manager would manage the sustainability reporting initiative for the entire organization, he or she can have significant contributions to the GRI reporting framework, particularly in the environmental category. With over 30 environmental indicators in the G3.1 framework and the construction and real estate sector supplement, the facility manager will find control or significant influence over the majority of environmental indicators. The facility manager's influence may not be confined to just the environmental category, as there are procurement, employment, customer health and safety, product labeling, and a number of other aspects and indicators under the social and financial reporting categories.

Table 5.2 is a sampling of environmental aspects and indicators that the facility manager may measure, monitor, and report. The indicators in Table 5.2 are composed of those that are core (shaded) and additional (unshaded). Core indicators have been identified in the GRI guidelines to be of interest to most stakeholders. Additional indicators represent emerging practice and may not be material to all organizations.

Table 5.2   The GRI environmental aspects and indicators most relevant to facility management

Environmental performance (EN)		
Aspect		Indicator
Materials	EN1	Materials used by weight or volume
	EN2	Percentage of materials that are recycled input materials
Energy	EN3	Direct energy consumption by the primary energy source
	EN4	Indirect energy consumption by the primary energy source
	EN5	Energy saved due to conservation and efficiency
	EN6	Initiatives to provide energy-efficient or renewable energy-based products and services
	EN7	Initiatives to reduce indirect energy consumption
Water	EN8	Total water withdrawal by the source
	EN9	Water sources significantly affected by withdrawal of water
	EN10	Percentage and total volume of water recycled and reused
Biodiversity	EN11	Location and size of land owned, leased, managed in, or adjacent to protected areas and of high biodiversity value outside protected areas
	EN12	Description of significant impacts of activities, products, and services on biodiversity in protected areas and areas of high biodiversity value outside protected areas
	EN13	Habitats protected or restored
	EN14	Strategies, current actions, and future plans for managing impacts on biodiversity
	EN15	Number of Red List species with habitats in areas affected by operations
Emissions, effluents, and waste	EN16	Total direct and indirect greenhouse gas emissions by weight
	EN17	Other relevant indirect greenhouse gas emissions by weight
	EN18	Initiatives to reduce greenhouse gas emissions and reductions achieved
	EN19	Emissions of ozone-depleting substances by weight
	EN20	NOx, SOx, and other significant air emission by type and weight
	EN21	Total water discharge by quality and destination
	EN22	Total weight of waste by type and disposal method
	EN23	Total number and volume of significant spills
	EN24	Weight of transported waste that is deemed hazardous
	EN25	Identification and quantification of water bodies affected by an organization's discharges of water and runoff
Products and services	EN26	Initiatives to mitigate environmental impacts of products and services, and extent of impact mitigation
Compliance	EN27	Percentage of products sold and their packaging materials that are reclaimed by category
	EN28	Monetary value of significant fines and total number of nonmonetary sanctions for noncompliance with environmental laws and regulations
Transport	EN29	Environmental impacts of transporting products and materials used for the organization's operations
Overall	EN30	Total environmental protection expenditures and investments

Using these and other environmental indicators, the facility manager is tasked with measurement, monitoring, and reporting of a number of key metrics that demonstrate support for the organization's external commitment to sustainability. They are responsible for collecting and monitoring that data, and using it to make intelligent choices in their next facility decision. These decisions affect future energy consumption, water use, waste generation and management, and the comfort, safety, and efficiency of the workforce. These decisions need to be made from an economic perspective, social perspective, and environmental perspective.

Building Management

This section includes a map of the environmental indicators (ENs) of the GRI reporting protocol relative to the building management aspect of the facility manager's role. These environmental indicators are closely related to how the facility manager manages the physical assets of an organization in sync with the corporate philosophy (CSR) of the organization.

GRI Environmental Indicators   Materials   EN1   EN2   EN22

EN1 and EN2 are indicators of the amount of material used by an organization, and the percentage of materials used that are recycled input materials. These indicators are focused on the organization's use of raw materials. EN2 is a strong indicator of an organization's commitment to using recycled material in the production of their products. These indicators would be most important to facility managers in industrial facilities that produce large volumes of products. The facility manager's role may be in collection, management, and disposal of waste products. Waste would be included under the emissions, effluents, and waste environmental indicator, EN22. Waste management in facilities can also be a major cost and environmental driver. Recognition of the issue of waste in facilities begins with the concept of minimization of the amount of material required to produce the product or to construct the work environment.

Environmental indicator EN1 is intended to draw attention to the amount of material used by any organization and conscious efforts made to reduce consumption of those materials. In facility management, one of the most significant sources of materials is the construction, renovation, and capital renewal of facilities and building systems. Another major source of workplace material consumption and waste generation includes paper, packaging, routine waste, food service waste, and purchasing, use, and disposal of hazardous materials, such as cleaning chemicals, lamps, and other specialty building components. Recycling is captured in environmental indicator EN2 and has become a popular and effective way to curtail workplace waste for products like paper, bottles, cans, and many other workplace byproducts.

Stakeholder education and support for recycling can be a positive driver for waste handling and recycling in facilities. Most individuals can positively relate the handling of workplace waste to their own person experiences. The handling and disposal of hazardous materials in facilities are regulation driven, and control and documentation of specialty service providers for waste handling are routine parts of facility management.

GRI Energy Indicators   Energy   EN3   EN4   EN5   EN6   EN7

In sustainable facility management, most of our attention and potential financial impact come from the way we deal with energy consumption. The environmental indicators are captured by EN3 and EN4, our direct and indirect energy consumption.

Generations of buildings were designed and built without much regard to energy consumption, primarily because energy was plentiful and inexpensive at the time they were built. In the United States, it wasn't until the energy crisis of the early 1970s that US designers paid much attention to the energy efficiency of buildings. Even when they did, the response was to find the simplest solution to the problem – close the building and provide total control of the indoor environment. While this may have saved a significant amount of energy, it led to other problems, particularly with regard to indoor air quality.

As energy costs continued to rise and the issue of unhealthy indoor environments began drawing attention, designers started to look at creating more energy-efficient buildings and harnessing the positive effects of integrating the indoor and outdoor environments to produce a more efficient and healthier indoor environment. Unfortunately, these two aspects of building operations are often at odds with each other, as the greater the influx of outdoor air, the greater the energy demand for heating and cooling. This requires much more complex building controls and highly trained operators to assure continued efficient performance.

The energy efficiency of buildings is not a tremendously complex thing to calculate. There is a relatively well-known metric that can be used worldwide and translated into either metric or English units (Peterson and Crowther, 2010). The common definition of the Energy Utilization Index (EUI) is as follows:

$$\frac{\text{Annual Building Energy Use} \left(\text{MJ or kBTUs} \right)}{\text{Building Area} \left(\text{square meters or square feet} \right)}$$

This represents the amount of energy used per unit of area of a building over a one-year period. It forms the basis of most of the major building energy calculations around the world. The amount of energy is usually derived from the amount of electricity and gas consumed in the heating and cooling of a building. Electricity (measured in watts or joules) and gas (measured in therms) is measured and converted to megajoules (MJ) or British Thermal Units (BTUs) over a period of time and divided by the area of the building. Typically, the gross building area is used, but other considerations are made for building features that may not be included in the gross area. The area of the building is not the only measure used to determine energy efficiency; often, energy used per unit produced, or energy per output, is a more effective way for some to evaluate their energy efficiency.

For buildings, the EUI is most often expressed in terms of the gross area of the building and the amount of site energy used. Site energy is defined as the amount of energy that crosses the property line. If site energy is used for the EUI calculation, it does not take into account the amount of electricity produced at the source (the power plant). The generation and transmission of electricity can often require three or more times as many units of electricity to be produced to deliver one unit at the point of use (the building), and it is referred to as source energy. Some EUI calculations are determined based on source energy.

If we wish to benchmark energy consumption across several geographic regions and in differing climates, the EUI is typically used as the baseline; it is then corrected for climate requirements through a normalization process of the data. It is also important when benchmarking to compare like data and to set parameters around building use, hours of operation, building population, types of energy demands, and many other factors. Benchmarking tools, such as the US Environmental Protection Agency's ENERGY STAR Portfolio Manager (www.energystar.gov), have a number of defined parameters that are reported in a consistent manner before two buildings can truly be compared or benchmarked against each other, and only site energy is used in determining the EUI.

In measuring and reporting energy consumption, it is important to consider both direct and indirect energy consumption, particularly when considering carbon emissions, as outlined in the "GRI Carbon (Emissions and Effluents) Indicators" section. Direct energy consumption is considered to be what an organization actually produces onsite. Examples of this would be a campus that has a central heating and cooling plant that produces its own energy for distribution to buildings. In this case, EUI remains the primary measure of efficiency since the calculation of energy consumption can be determined by converting steam, electricity, gas, and other forms of fuel to MJ or kBTUs (thousands of BTUs).

The other important measure is indirect energy consumption: that which comes from offsite and is purchased from a producer. This is often the most easily measured type of energy because it is required to be accurately measured at the point of delivery. These terms become particularly important when we discuss carbon emissions.

Facility managers are usually the purchasers of energy. Therefore, they control the measurement and distribution of the purchase, delivery and consumption of energy throughout facilities. As a purchaser, the facility manager may have limited control over how to manage and reduce the source and cost of energy. However, many facility managers are very skilled at aggregating their purchasing power through bulk purchasing agreements and shared cost-savings arrangements with service providers. Careful watch over time of use, peak demand, and consumption of electrical power are all areas the facility manager can use to influence the purchase, delivery and consumption of energy.

The additional indicators EN5, EN6, and EN7 deal with the quantification of energy savings (EN5), and the promotion of sustainability initiatives within a facility that lead to direct and indirect energy savings (EN6 and EN7). These indicators have a high level of materiality for facility managers and form the basis of many of the day-to-day drivers of sustainable facility management.

Reducing demand through energy savings initiatives, energy-efficient purchasing, and occupant education provides ample opportunity for energy reduction.

The facility manager's greatest contribution to energy management comes through the following:

- Effective energy purchasing
- Controlling and curtailing demand
- Installation and management of energy-efficient building systems and components
- Influencing energy behavior.

GRI Water and Waste Indicators   Water and waste EN8 EN9 EN10 EN21 EN25

The environmental indicators of the GRI quantify the amount of water used (EN8) and the total amount of water discharged by quality and destination (EN21). The use of water in the workplace is a significant factor in our overall use of water as a natural resource. The use of water in the workplace can generally be quantified into three primary areas: domestic, process, and irrigation.

Domestic water in the workplace includes water for washing and showering and for waste disposal. Quantification of the amount of water we use in the workplace is based on the population mix between men and women and the overall size of the workforce. Reasonably well-established quantities of water for this use are estimated and included in most plumbing codes. Washroom facilities are designed and built to these norms, and the facility manager is then charged with keeping the building systems and fixtures in good repair to reduce overall water consumption. Kitchen and laundry facilities are also critical in evaluating and reducing water consumption, particularly in hospitality and healthcare facilities. The introduction of low-flow toilets, waterless and low-flow urinals, and low-flow lavatory fixtures has led to significant reductions in domestic water use in buildings worldwide over the last several years.

The second major category of water use in buildings is the process water used in the heating and cooling of facilities. Facilities with open-loop cooling systems use a significant amount of water to make up for evaporation and water loss in cooling towers. Open- and closed-loop heating and cooling systems also use chemicals to prevent corrosion of the piping systems. These chemicals can also present an environmental challenge to facility managers, and chemical treatment systems can also be expensive to operate and maintain. In tropical and other traditionally high-temperature climates, recapture of cooling condensate water can be an effective technique for the reduction of water use and for increased efficiencies gained from the capture and reuse of cool water.

The third and often most significant use of water in facilities is from irrigation. The use of plantings to provide pleasing surroundings in our buildings is often a major factor in attracting and retaining workers and providing an inviting environment for visitors. However, the cost of water for landscaping is high in terms of the amount of water we divert from local aquifers and take away from much-needed domestic use. Although the cost of water is not necessarily high in many areas of the world, authorities predict it will be an increasing problem that may soon become a cost driver in facilities.

An Australian study of water use in buildings was undertaken to determine if water use related to office and public buildings could be benchmarked and appropriate hours of use, water management practices, exterior water features, and a number of different factors determined (Bannister *et al.*, 2005). The average consumption intensity of both public and office buildings in the Australian study was 3.34 kl/m²/year. Interestingly, this benchmark for buildings did not vary significantly with changes in building density. The other significant finding was that a best practice target of 2.0 kl/m²/year was achievable (a two-thirds reduction from the baseline). The study concluded that although the baseline water use would vary depending on where you were located in the world, the consumption level versus the best practice target savings would remain proportional. The study compared favorably in scale to the UK Watermark program.

Environmental indicators EN9 and 10 deal with the water affected by withdrawals (EN9) and the percentage of total volume of water recycled and reused (EN10). While the water affected by withdrawals is most likely a local environmental protection issue, the percentage of recycled and reused water would be of direct interest to the facility manager. Environmental indicator EN25 deals with identifying the protection status and biodiversity value of water bodies that are affected by an organization's water discharges and runoff.

GRI Site Issues (Biodiversity) Indicators

Site issues (biodiversity)	EN11	EN12	EN13	EN14	EN15

The site issues in the GRI environmental indicators are measures of the facility sites that are owned and operated by the organization relative to protected environmental areas or areas of high biodiversity value (EN11), and the significant impacts of activities, products, or services in relation to these areas (EN12). The facility manager who has responsibility for sites adjacent to environmentally sensitive areas that would require control of runoff, effluent control, and sensitivity to plants, trees, and wildlife must incorporate measures to protect adjacent areas from organizational activities. Many of the building sustainability rating systems have points or credits that deal with site issues and environmentally sensitive areas adjacent to building sites. The additional environmental site indicators EN13, EN14, and EN15 deal with the protection of habitats, strategies for protection of habitats in future expansions, and protection of specific protected species, respectively.

GRI Carbon (Emissions and Effluents) Indicators

Carbon (emissions and effluents)	EN16	EN17	EN18	EN19	EN20	EN23	EN24

Greenhouse gas emissions are one of the most significant drivers of sustainability efforts around the world. The GRI protocol captures greenhouse gas emissions primarily through direct and indirect measurement (EN16), and other greenhouse gas emissions (EN17). Since buildings account for a significant amount of our greenhouse gas emissions, primarily through our use of purchased and onsite energy production, the influence of the facility manager on carbon emissions is significant. The Greenhouse Gas Protocol Initiative (World Resources Institute (WRI) and WBCSD, 2004) provides a methodology for measuring and reporting greenhouse gas emissions. The greenhouse gas emission protocol consists of three primary components, as shown in Figure 5.3.

While Scope 1 and 2 emissions comprise a significant portion of most organizations' carbon footprint, they are also the most easily determined. Other emissions (Scope 3) include those produced by commuting, producing, and selling products and services, waste, and a wide variety of other emissions. Scope 3 emissions are the most complex and

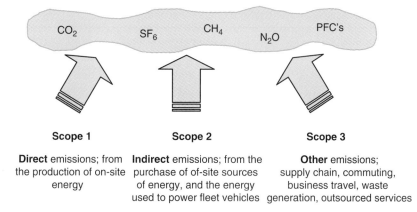

Figure 5.3 Three scopes of greenhouse gas emissions (adapted from WRI and WBCSD, 2004).

difficult to measure since they often include measurement of production and transportation of goods that are not under the direct control of the measuring organization.

In any greenhouse gas measurement activity, it is important to set boundaries in order to make measurement and reporting possible. These boundaries include important factors such as what parts of the organization to measure (organizational boundaries) and what greenhouse gas–generating activities to measure (operational boundaries). Measuring greenhouse gas emissions is somewhat more complex than measuring energy consumption in that the source of the energy and how it was produced becomes important. In the determination of EUI, we typically do not take the source of the energy into account since we are only measuring at the point of consumption. When measuring greenhouse gas emissions, the source and type of power generation are important. The producer's fuel sources and the efficiency of the grid in its ability to transmit power from producer to consumer influence greenhouse gas emissions and carbon footprint.

Table 5.3 represents a typical boundary that would be set from the facility manager's perspective. The dotted line represents metrics that would fall under the facility manager's responsibilities relative to onsite and purchased energy, and the operation of fleet vehicles. Depending on the facility manager's role in sustainability reporting for the organization, additional measurements of carbon emissions might include business travel, commuting, and supply chain and outsourced service emissions.

The reduction in Scope 3 emissions becomes the most problematic for facility managers. Their influence over the process of emissions reduction becomes an issue of how much of their organization's commuting and purchasing processes they are able to influence. Environmental indicator EN18 is an "initiative-based" metric that deals with the ability

Table 5.3 Drawing organizational and operational boundaries

Upstream emissions	Corporate emissions	Downstream emissions
Scope 2 emissions	Scope 1 emissions	Scope 3 emissions
Production of electricity consumed	Onsite fuel combustion	Distribution of products
Production of raw materials	Company-owned vehicles	Retail
Processing of purchased materials	Business travel	Product use
Transportation of purchased materials	Employee commuting	Product disposal
	Outsourced corporate support services	

to introduce initiatives to reduce greenhouse gas emissions. One of the primary reduction strategies is to reduce direct and indirect fuel consumption. Facility managers would most likely be directly involved in the measurement and development of reduction strategies for greenhouse gas emissions. Environmental indicators EN19, EN20, and EN23 deal with other emissions, such as ozone-depleting substances, NO, SO, and the amount of significant spills generated by the organization. Environmental indicator EN24 deals with the transportation waste that is deemed hazardous.

GRI Products and Services, and Compliance, Indicators

Products and services, and compliance   EN26   EN27   EN28

Environmental indicators EN26 and EN27 deal with the downstream aspects of products sold and services provided. These indicators would be most relevant to organizations that have emissions profiles similar to those of the auto manufacturers depicted in Figure 5.1. For these types of organizations, initiatives to reduce the negative downstream effects of their products or services on the environment are captured by EN26. EN27 is a measurement of the packaging materials used in the provision of products that are reclaimed from the waste stream. Environmental indicator EN28 quantifies the monetary value of significant fines and a number of nonmonetary sanctions for noncompliance with environmental laws and regulations.

GRI Transport and Overall Indicators   Transport and overall indicators   EN29   EN30

The final environmental indicators that are included in the GRI framework include measures of significant environmental impacts from the transport of goods and the workforce (EN29) and the total environmental protection expenditures by type (EN30). Quantification of the environmental impacts of transportation of members of the workforce could include issues that are monitored and measured by the facility manager, depending on his or her role in the organization and whether they are drivers of the sustainability strategies of the organization. The quantification of the total value of environmental protection expenditures will also depend on the facility manager's role in, and the environmental profile of, the organization.

Workplace Management

This section addresses the role of the facility manager relative to workplace management, and it is driven from a GRI reporting standpoint to the social aspects of the GRI protocol and the triple bottom line. In addition to measuring and monitoring the building-related environmental aspects and indicators that have been listed in this chapter, the facility manager is in a position to make significant contributions to the health and well-being of the workforce.

Management of the work environment in a sustainable and cost-effective manner has been a performance driver for facility managers since long before the advent of green buildings. Many large organizations have held the health and safety of the workforce uppermost on its priority list for decades. The attention brought to the workplace over the past several years by the green building movement has reinforced the idea that a healthy workforce is more productive and better for an organization's bottom line, even in organizations that are not driven by profit.

These primary drivers in workplace management are the most important in maintaining sustainable facilities:

- Indoor environmental quality
- Effective space management.

The quality of the indoor environment affects workplace performance on an individual level. There are six primary human and environmental factors that lead to high-quality indoor environments:

- Temperature and relative humidity
- Sound management
- Lighting
- Aesthetics
- Ergonomics
- Social interaction in the workplace.

While it is not reasonable to assume that every employee in the work environment will have the same level of satisfaction with a fixed approach to these factors, high-quality work environments pay attention to each of these factors. Building technology systems allow us to control these factors in a manner that will maximize customer satisfaction and productivity of the workforce. Sustainable workplaces consider each of these factors and work to balance the needs of the individual with the energy and resource demands of the facility.

The need for more effective use of space has been accentuated over the last few years as many global companies have downsized their facilities and sought greater efficiency through higher occupancy densities. Many of these changes have been driven by economics, but they may also fit well with sustainability initiatives. Less space to manage leads to a smaller carbon footprint. There may be some societal issues in the workplace that need to be overcome that have to do with the relationship between the size of a person's workspace and his or her position in the organization's hierarchy. Improvements in aesthetics, amenities, and technology have offset many of the drawbacks of smaller work spaces.

Life-Cycle Management

A renewed focus on the life cycle of buildings and systems can also support efforts toward more sustainable facilities. Using future energy savings to offset higher initial costs can encourage more sustainable contributions to the bottom line. Choosing building materials and systems that are more durable and have longer service lives can enhance sustainability efforts.

> Although most facility managers would argue that they have always emphasized life cycle over short-term solutions, the truth is that, in general, we may not have been as effective in convincing upper management in our organizations to take the long-term view in making facility operational, repair, and replacement choices.

More in-depth knowledge of financial goals of an organization can enhance a facility manager's ability to make the business case for sustainable initiatives. Energy efficient retrofits and building system upgrades that yield long-term savings can be very effective ways to promote sustainable facility management and increase financial returns. The ability of the facility manager to look beyond simple financial terms, such as payback period and simple return on investment, can yield significant cost savings that might not otherwise have been chosen. The ability of the facility manager to quantify and help assess risk can also help pass the level of scrutiny on sustainability and routine facility management initiatives. The ability to show the consequences of *not* taking action on operational and maintenance issues is critical in life-cycle management. Finally, the ability to show alignment with organizational strategies and goals and the ability to align sustainable initiatives to make the business case for the intangible benefits that support CSR, particularly the social and environmental intangibles, are valuable skills.

Measurement and Monitoring

Above all else, the facility manager's role in measuring and managing the resources that go into the operations and maintenance of facilities is perhaps his or her greatest contribution to sustainable facilities.

Improvement in building performance is dependent on occupant cooperation and assistance, and proper management procedures that promote building efficiency; the facility manager is the steward of the workplace environment and generally leads the charge in occupant education.

Turning off lights and appliances that are not in use, reducing the amount of water used in facilities, and proper use of recycling systems require significant continuing education and monitoring of processes. Facility managers also manage the processes for measurement and monitoring of workplace environmental efforts, and they need to strike the right balance between occupant satisfaction and the delivery of efficient buildings.

Measurement of energy use is the primary target of most sustainable building initiatives due to its immediate impact and potential for significant financial savings. However, improvements in measurement science are needed to be able to quantify the energy performance of buildings. The primary obstacle in older buildings is the ability to meter electrical use. Over the past 20 years, many buildings were renovated to accommodate technology improvements, such as data centers. Unfortunately, separate measurement of the energy required to power data centers was not necessarily considered when they were installed. It is no longer sufficient to provide one meter to measure electrical consumption at the entry point of the facility. Metering plans with multiple data points are required in order to isolate different building systems. Metering plans provide the facility manager with the ability to isolate building systems and target efficiency improvements at the most inefficient systems.

Data management has become a significant challenge in existing facilities. Along with data management, processes for selecting and monitoring the most important performance metrics are needed. Most modern building technology systems have capabilities for monitoring and measuring a vast number of performance metrics that are usually not present in older buildings. The ability to strategize on appropriate metrics is a critical first step. Once the appropriate metrics are chosen, continual monitoring and reporting processes are required to properly manage reduction initiatives.

Newly designed and built facilities offer significant opportunities for the installation of monitoring and reporting systems. Building management and energy management systems are now commonplace in new buildings and should provide metrics, methods, and tools for real-time monitoring of energy and water consumption and for monitoring key elements that affect the indoor environment. However, the most significant improvements in building metrics may come from existing buildings. Existing building monitoring can be as simple as monitoring energy consumption through billing and invoicing processes, or installing meters and measuring devices to isolate resource use in targeted areas of the facility.

The facility manager creates the operating and capital budget framework for facilities and should consider measurement and monitoring programs that will provide the information and metrics for prioritizing sustainability initiatives. Appropriate knowledge of metering plans and program implementation techniques is critical for the facility manager and his or her staff. Improvements in measuring and monitoring systems should include the ability to monitor plug loads, lighting, major appliances, and heating, ventilation, and cooling.

Facility managers are in a position to apply the triple bottom line to building performance, in order to prioritize and seek the most important metrics that demonstrate building performance. Those metrics should not be confined to energy only, but should also include building performance metrics, system performance metrics, material performance metrics, and material production metrics; this methodology leads to an integrated approach to building measuring and monitoring systems. If these systems are properly integrated into a performance management system, the measurement and monitoring function in a facility should be able to provide real-time, or near real-time, monitoring capabilities that allow the facility manager to make adjustments for changes in occupancy, upcoming events, emergencies, and routine capital and operating budget cycles.

Summary and Conclusions

Over the past several years, there has been an emphasis on the design and construction of sustainable or green buildings. The design community has pushed for a greater focus on sustainable communities, energy efficiency, resource conservation, and the quality of the living and work environment. This emphasis has been quite successful in getting us to think in terms of efficient and high-performance facilities. However, if we are able to shift the emphasis from the features and characteristics of the facility to how it is operated and managed over its life cycle, we will be able to make far more significant changes by effectively managing building systems.

There are also significant gains to be made by looking at the workplace in its totality, and matching workplace management strategies with the mission and vision of the organization. The facility manager is uniquely positioned to understand the philosophy, mission, and values that drive their organization's actions. If they are attuned to organizational drivers, they will be able to adapt and align the operation of their facilities to the organizational philosophy and commitment to CSR. Whether that commitment is strong or weak, the facility manager should be able to navigate the waters of his or her work environment and produce building operating protocols that meet the social and environmental drivers of the organization while operating in an economically efficient manner.

From a life-cycle perspective, the facility manager is one of the most influential individuals in creating an efficient and productive work environment. During a building's life cycle, there will be significant capital and operating dollars spent. These dollars far outweigh the amount spent on the design and construction of facilities. The FM's position in the management of the facility life cycle, the magnitude of funding involved, and the ability to align with the organization's commitment to the triple bottom line can far outweigh the impact of a well-designed and built facility. It is in the management of the facility that the greatest impact lies, not necessarily in how it was built. There is no doubt that a combination of carefully considered green design and construction and sustainable facility management would produce the greatest return for any organization. However, in order to get to that combination, we should place more emphasis on how we manage sustainable facilities. In following each of these three key elements of the contribution of the facility manager to sustainable facilities – building management, workplace management, and life-cycle management – we will be able to produce efficient, effective, and environmentally friendly work environments and be able to demonstrate the value of the facility manager's contribution through sustainability reporting.

References

Bannister, P., Munzinger, M., and Bloomfield, C. (2005). *Water benchmarks for offices and public buildings*. Belconnen, Australia: Exergy Australia Pty Ltd.

Carbon Disclosure Project. (2012). *Guidance for first-time responders to CDP*. London: Carbon Disclosure Project.

Epstein, M. (2008). *Making sustainability work*. San Francisco: Greenleaf Publishing and Berrett-Koehler.

Esty, D., and Winston, A. (2006). *Green to gold*. New Haven, CT: Yale University Press.

Global Reporting Initiative. (2000–2011). *GRI sustainability reporting guidelines G3.1 – reference sheet*. Amsterdam: Global Reporting Initiative.

Global Reporting Initiative. (2011). *Sustainability reporting guidelines (G3.1)*. Amsterdam: Global Reporting Initiative.

National Science and Technology Council, Committee on Technology. (2008). *Federal research and development agenda for net-zero energy, high-performance green buildings*. Washington, DC: Executive Office of the President.

Peterson, K., and Crowther, H. (2010). Building EUI's. Paper presented at High Performance Buildings, summer meeting of the American Society of Heating, Refrigerating and Air-Conditioning Engineers (ASHRAE), Atlanta, GA.

United Nations. (1987). Our common future. Available at: http://www.un-documents.net/ocf-02.htm#I (accessed 23 June 2013).

UN Global Compact Office. (2011). *Corporate sustainability in the world economy: United Nations Global Compact*. UN Global Compact Office.

World Resources Institute (WRI) and World Business Council for Sustainable Development (WBCSD). (2004). *The greenhouse gas protocol: a corporate accounting and reporting standard*. Washington, DC, and Geneva: WRI and WBCSD.

Internet References

Carbon Disclosure Project: www.cdproject.net, London, UK

Global Reporting Initiative: www.globalreporting.org, Amsterdam, The Netherlands

International Organization for Standardization: www.iso.org, Geneva, Switzerland

UN Global Compact: www.unglobalcompact.org, New York, USA

US Environmental Protection Agency, ENERGY STAR Portfolio Manager: www.energystar.gov, Washington, DC, USA

World Business Council for Sustainable Development: www.wbcsd.org, Geneva, Switzerland

World Resources Institute: www.wri.org, Washington, DC, USA

Emergency Preparedness and Business Continuity

Robert Friedmann[1] and Bob Hayes[2]

[1] Georgia State University, Atlanta, GA
[2] Security Executive Council, Marietta, GA

Business Continuity Program (BCP) Management

Corporations face threat vulnerability from several sources: natural disasters, man-made disasters, technical malfunctions, data integrity penetration, name or product reputation damage, unstable markets, or any combination of the above. Each of these threats could result in temporary halting of operations or even a complete shutdown and company collapse. It is important for facility management (FM) professionals to assess these threats, prepare for them, and have plans in place to ensure uninterrupted business operations. The business continuity program

The authors acknowledge that material used for this chapter is based on proprietary information that has been licensed to the Security Executive Council. A non-exclusive limited license was granted to the authors to use this material for this chapter. Authorization does not constitute a transfer of intellectual property rights. This material remains the intellectual property of the Security Executive Council. The authors further acknowledge that beyond this limited use authorization, this material may not be sold, copied, reproduced electronically or by any other means, transferred, utilized in any manner other than internal to the licensee's entity/organization/agency or presented outside the licensee's entity/organization/agency without first seeking and obtaining written authorization from the Security Executive Council. This material may not be integrated in whole or in part into any commercial offering or utilized as the foundation of any commercial effort of the entity/organization without first seeking and obtaining written authorization from the Security Executive Council.

International Facility Management, First Edition. Kathy O. Roper and Lisa J. Borello.
© 2014 John Wiley & Sons, Ltd. Published 2014 by John Wiley & Sons, Ltd.

(BCP) is based on the principle that the better and more comprehensive the plan, the more systematic the prevention efforts; the more thorough the preparedness efforts, the more extensive the training; and the more efficacious the response, the better the recovery. This chapter outlines BCP planning principles that address prevention and mitigation, preparedness, training, response, incident notification, and recovery; this framework can be adapted to a variety of organizations and can be utilized by facility managers in executing comprehensive business continuity and emergency response plans. The purpose of BCP is to offer business continuity principles in emergency situations. If challenged with a critical incident, companies must be able to respond in the quickest and best way possible for their employees, customers, business, and external stakeholders, *protecting people and assets while expediting the resumption of normal operations.*

Authorities and Legislative Requirements

BCP should be maintained as a living document and promulgated under the authority of the local government. In the United States, the president (and relevant federal legislation) sets this legislation. Planning must also include NFPA 1600 (in the United States) or CSAZ1600 (in Canada). *The NFPA1600 incorporates a risk-based, all-hazards approach that integrates emergency management and BCPs for a total program approach.* Each local government's fire protection codes should be fully incorporated into the BCP in order to meet the risk demands prevalent in each locale.

The elements of BCP cover the four pillars of effective emergency management – prevention and mitigation, preparedness, response, and recovery – which are commensurate with the risks established for hazard identification, risk assessment, and business impact analysis. The objectives of BCP are protection of life, protection of the environment, protection of company assets, and promotion of resumption to normal operations.

Developing a BCP

A policy should be established that clearly defines the mission and vision statements, and roles and responsibilities of the individuals charged with executing the BCP should also be established. An effective records management process, which includes the documentation and maintenance of all logs, records, and activities related to its BCP, is also required and is typically the responsibility of facility management departments.

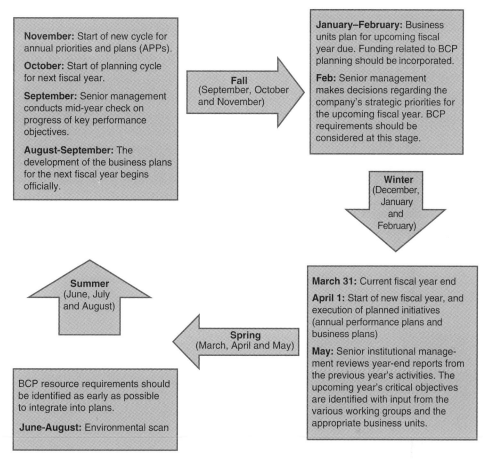

November: Start of new cycle for annual priorities and plans (APPs).

October: Start of planning cycle for next fiscal year.

September: Senior management conducts mid-year check on progress of key performance objectives.

August-September: The development of the business plans for the next fiscal year begins officially.

Fall (September, October and November)

January–February: Business units plan for upcoming fiscal year due. Funding related to BCP planning should be incorporated.

Feb: Senior management makes decisions regarding the company's strategic priorities for the upcoming fiscal year. BCP requirements should be considered at this stage.

Winter (December, January and February)

Summer (June, July and August)

BCP resource requirements should be identified as early as possible to integrate into plans.

June-August: Environmental scan

Spring (March, April and May)

March 31: Current fiscal year end

April 1: Start of new fiscal year, and execution of planned initiatives (annual performance plans and business plans)

May: Senior institutional management reviews year-end reports from the previous year's activities. The upcoming year's critical objectives are identified with input from the various working groups and the appropriate business units.

Figure 6.1   BCP planning cycle.

Developing a BCP Team

Defining roles and responsibilities is a key component of developing and executing an effective crisis management strategy. In addition to the input of senior management, successful execution of a BCP requires a Program Coordinator, Advisory Committee, Crisis Management Team, Incident Management Team, and Local Response Team. Facility management should ensure that, irrespective of other responsibilities, there are defined roles, responsibilities, and authority for ensuring that an emergency management program and BCP are established, maintained, and reviewed in accordance with the BCP planning cycle, which is shown in Figure 6.1.

A distinct *Program Coordinator* ensures the preparation, implementation, evaluation, maintenance, and revision of the program. An Advisory Committee, led by the Program Coordinator, provides guidance and advice to improve the program. The Committee should include representation from functional subject matter experts (SMEs) potentially impacted by identified hazards and threats. Consideration should be given to including other public or private stakeholders, vendors, and community representatives. It is suggested that provision be made for cross-sector representation on the committee. A list of those who should be included in any one sector depends on the size and complexity of the entity.

A *Crisis Management Team* (CMT) includes senior executives who provide guidance and make decisions regarding policy, procedure, and finances as they relate to the management of critical incidents. The CMT may be led by the functional leader of a company's Security Department or the Facility Management executive. All CMT Primary Members must have an identified back-up member from their respective functions if they are not able to participate in a CMT meeting. Other relevant external stakeholders may be brought in to support the CMT as required.

An *Incident Management Team* (IMT) actively manages critical incidents that extensively threaten employees, assets, and brand reputation from the corporate office. This group consists of SMEs from each critical business function, and its leader may be from within the company's Facility and/or Security Department. All IMT Primary Members must have an identified back-up member from their respective function if they are not able to participate. Other relevant external stakeholders may be brought in to support the IMT as required.

The *Local Response Team* (LRT) responds to local critical incidents that extensively threaten employees, assets, and brand reputation. This group consists of local SMEs from each critical business function and may be led by the local leader of a company's Facility Management and/or Security Department. All LRT Primary Members must have an identified back-up member from their respective function if they are not able to participate. Other relevant external stakeholders may be brought in to support the LRT as required.

CMT, IMT, and LRT Members' Roles and Responsibilities

The CMT Lead organizes and calls meetings. This lead individual will determine which active members and SMEs will participate in the CMT meetings. Additional duties of the Lead include the following:

- Aligns the CMT on roles and responsibilities at the first meeting
- Keeps minutes and tracks commitments
- Drives for team alignment on action steps when immediate incident response is required
- Works in collaboration with IMT Lead to determine when it is appropriate to notify or convene the CMT
- Helps company determine other internal and external stakeholders to represent business units as decision makers
- Organizes future meetings
- Creates and distributes communications to correct audiences.

The IMT Lead will be the individual responsible for evaluating incident levels and organizing and calling meetings. This Lead will determine which active members and SMEs will participate in the IMT meetings, and aligns the IMT on roles and responsibilities at the first meeting. Additional duties of the IMT Lead are as follows:

- Keeps minutes and tracks commitments
- Drives for team alignment on action steps when immediate incident response is required
- Works in collaboration with the LRT Lead (if necessary) to determine appropriate incident communication to the CMT Lead
- Helps company determine other internal and external stakeholders to represent business units as decision makers
- Organizes future meetings
- Creates and distributes communications to correct audiences.

CMT, IMT, and LRT Members will participate in requested crisis management meetings. They may also be asked to join other meetings as "optional attendees." Additional duties of all team members include the following:

- Helps company determine other internal or external stakeholders to represent business units as decision makers
- Participates in the identification of SME needs
- Identifies potential escalation of circumstances
- Provides communications of incident within their function.

SMEs contribute expert opinion and offer strategic options. They should highlight negative ramifications prior to plan implementation, and assist the CMT and/or IMT as required to determine the correct decision makers in an ongoing incident.

Although the Program Coordinator has final authority in deciding the course of the program through its day-to-day administration, major decisions should be made in consultation with the Advisory Committee. The Program Coordinator and the Advisory Committee should be in agreement concerning priorities and resource allocation in the day-to-day operation of the program.

Program Review

An organization conducts a periodic review of the BCP based on the goals, objectives, and evaluation of the program in order to continuously improve the plan's ability to accomplish its objectives. A program review serves to confirm that the company's emergency management program and BCP are fully implemented and meet its objectives.

A periodic evaluation is beneficial to program management, authorities, and other stakeholders who have an interest in the program by confirming where the program is working correctly and where improvements are required. Information compiled from an evaluation can be used to assess program performance and aids in setting priorities for program improvements. Program evaluation helps to provide justification for recommended changes to a program and supports continuous improvement.

Business Continuity Planning Continuum

Figure 6.2 highlights the four interdependent risk-based functions of BCP: prevention and mitigation of, preparedness for, response to, and recovery from emergencies. These functions can be undertaken sequentially or concurrently, and they are interdependent. The inner circle includes all of the elements that influence the development of the BCP and also emphasizes the fact that the BCP is a living document that is continuously improved and adjusted, for instance as lessons are learned through responses and exercises, or as a changing risk environment is integrated.

To further illustrate this point, Figure 6.1 highlights a typical BCP planning cycle, reiterating the requirement to review the plan at planned intervals, not just when an incident occurs.

Prevention and Mitigation

The key task involved with this BCP component is to identify and develop activities, tasks, programs, and systems that are intended to avoid emergencies or stop such events from occurring. This should include a process involving hazard identification, risk assessment, a business impact analysis (BIA), and a vendor resiliency questionnaire.

Hazard Identification

Hazards are typically grouped into three categories: natural, human caused, and technological. Naturally occurring hazards include earthquakes, tsunamis, fire, flood, hurricanes, snow, pandemics, and so on. A human-caused event includes a hazardous material spill or release, terrorism, theft, fraud, workplace violence, sabotage, an explosion, flammable liquid, or flammable gas. Technology-caused events involve computers; hardware, software, or application (internal or external) malfunction or breakdown; and so on. These hazards can then be plotted on a matrix and heat map to visually illustrate the top hazards for which mitigation strategies should be implemented.

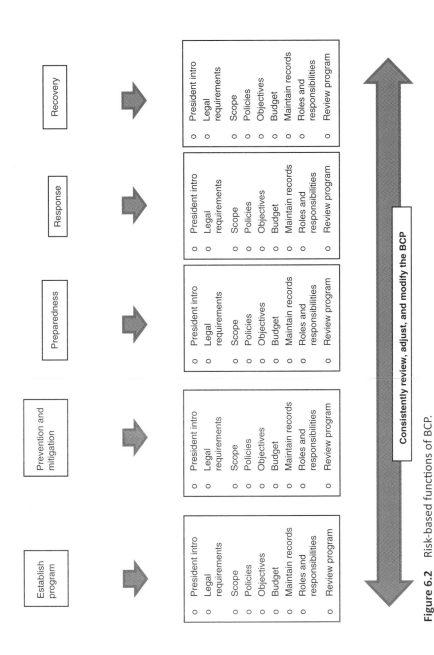

Figure 6.2 Risk-based functions of BCP.

Business Impact Analysis

Once risks have been identified, any organizational impacts that could result from an interruption of normal operations should be examined in a BIA. The completion of a BIA can be broken into the following steps:

Step 1: Identify critical processes. Business critical processes should be identified and documented. They could include purchasing, manufacturing, supply chain, sales, distribution, accounts receivable, accounts payable, payroll, information technology (IT), and research and development. Once the critical processes and related interdependencies are identified, an analysis of each can be made.

Step 2: Determine maximum allowable outage and recovery time objectives. Determine how long a process can be nonfunctional before impacts become unacceptable, then determine how soon the process should be restored, and determine different recovery time objectives according to the time of year (year-end, tax filing, etc.).

Step 3: Identify resources required for resumption and recovery. Such resources can include personnel, technology hardware and software (including telecommunications), specialized equipment, general office supplies, facility or office space, and critical and vital business records. Identifying, backing up, and storing critical and vital business records in a safe and accessible location are essential prerequisites for an effective BCP.

The risk assessment and BIA provide the foundation on which the organization's BCP will rest, as strategies will be formulated and plans will be developed to meet the needs identified in them. These analyses should be repeated on an annual basis at minimum, as well as in response to significant changes to the organization's operating environment.

Vendor Resiliency Questionnaire

Most companies are reliant on outsourced vendors to support its operations. Therefore, these outsourced vendors are key members of a company's BCP. It is critical to obtain information on their BCP readiness. This will provide a company with reassurance that the vendor is performing its diligence within the four pillars of its BCP program to an acceptable minimum standard.

Preparedness

The objective of planning activities associated with preparedness is to have an effective and coordinated approach to BCP and operational readiness. These should include the following:

- Maintaining a level of sustainable capacity to meet the goals outlined in individual business unit BCP plans, based on priorities, needs analysis, and capability requirements
- Conducting or participating in exercises to test and implement specific incident plans based on identified top risks
- Participating in training of key stakeholders with respect to business continuity planning
- Incorporating lessons learned and best practices derived from actual events, training, and exercises into the BCP process
- Providing post-exercise and post-event information to key stakeholders related to continuous improvement of the BCP
- Putting in place any required service-level agreements (SLAs), memoranda of understanding (MOU), and mutual assistance agreements with external stakeholders to ensure that services and/or facilities, as well as equipment, are secured in an emergency
- Procuring supplies and resources (e.g. to operate an Emergency Operations Center (EOC), provide an emergency stockpile, or ensure system redundancy).

Mutual Aid and Mutual Assistance

The term *mutual aid/mutual assistance agreement* includes cooperative assistance agreements, service-level agreements, intergovernmental compacts, or other terms commonly used for the sharing of resources. Mutual aid/mutual assistance agreements between entities are an effective means to obtain resources and should be developed whenever possible. Mutual aid/mutual assistance agreements are the means for one entity to provide resources, facilities, services, and other required support to another entity during an incident. Each entity should be party to a mutual aid/mutual assistance agreement with appropriate entities from which they expect to receive, or to which they expect to provide, assistance during an incident. This normally includes all neighboring or nearby entities, as well as relevant government, private sector, and nongovernmental organizations.

Mutual aid/mutual assistance agreements should be developed in consultation with the parties involved, set in writing, and reviewed by legal counsel. They should define liability, include detailed funding and cost arrangements, and be signed by responsible individuals. At a minimum, mutual aid/mutual assistance agreements should include the following elements or provisions:

- Definitions of key terms used in the agreement
- Roles and responsibilities of individual parties
- Procedures for requesting and providing assistance
- Procedures, authorities, and rules for payment, reimbursement, and allocation of costs

- Notification procedures
- Protocols for interoperable communications
- Relationships with other agreements among entities
- Employment standards and occupational health, and safety and workers' compensation coverage
- Treatment of liability and immunity
- Recognition of qualifications and certifications
- Sharing agreements, as required.

Communication Systems

Telecommunication and other communication systems should support all components of the program, in order to notify and update key internal and external stakeholders with an update regarding the incident. These systems can include the following:

- Wireline, wireless, and satellite telephones
- Pagers
- Fax machines
- Computer systems and networks, including personal digital assistants (PDAs), the company intranet, and external websites
- Automated, purchased, or hosted systems and services that can simultaneously send and/or verify
- Receipt of messages to telephone and computer devices
- Two-way radios operating on public, private, or amateur radio frequencies
- Public radio and television systems, including provision for interrupting broadcasts with emergency
- Messages, or superimposed messages on current programming
- Sirens and other outside warning devices
- Computerized incident management systems for sharing operational communications.

Redundancy in communication systems is essential in emergencies since normal operations may be non-operational.

Training

Training is an essential element of BCP. Those who perform tasks related to any aspect of the company's BCP are expected to be competent as a result of appropriate education, training, and experience. Experience is the key to effectiveness, and training prior to an emergency is required to ensure that experience because emergencies are not routine. Training or instruction should be conducted at all levels of the organization, including senior management, and they should be specific to emergency management and business continuity duties and responsibilities, as determined by a training needs assessment. Regular duties and responsibilities can include voluntary or additional responsibilities assumed on behalf of the organization. During the development of this component of the BCP, an individual should be assigned responsibility for developing and supporting a training plan or schedule. The training plan should consider the training and information needs of employees, contractors, managers, and those with an emergency response role identified in the BCP. Examples of training may include workshops, webinars, conference calls, internal or external courses, and industry-specific seminars.

Exercises

An exercise is a focused practice activity that places the participants in a simulated situation and required them to function in the capacity that would be expected of them in a real event. Its purpose is to promote preparedness by testing policies and plans and by training personnel.

Exercises should be designed using specific objectives to validate plans, test systems, and provide personnel with an opportunity to practice assigned roles in the plan. Exercise results identify plan gaps and limitations and are used to improve and revise the plans.

An exercise plan that schedules future exercises should be developed to ensure the following:

- Test and evaluate plans, policies, and procedures
- Reveal planning weaknesses
- Reveal gaps in resources
- Improve organizational coordination and communications
- Clarify roles and responsibilities
- Improve individual performance
- Satisfy regulatory requirements
- Participation is maximized
- Teamwork and partnerships are fostered

The exercise schedule should be based on organizational needs, current key hazards or threats facing the organization, and legislative requirements. Exercises should be conducted when there are additions, deletions, or revisions are made to the plan; there have been significant changes in key personnel who are responsible for implementing the plan; there have been changes to physical resources (e.g. facilities and equipment) identified in the plan; and/or there have been changes in the nature or type of risks that can have an effect on the type of response.

Exercises can be designed to test individual essential elements, inter-related elements, or the entire plan(s). They can take many forms, such as drills, tabletop exercises, full-scale exercises, and functional exercises. Exercises should be planned and conducted taking the following into consideration:

- The scenario should reflect reality as far as is practical
- The scenario should be based on the risk assessment
- Key stakeholders should participate
- Resources can be deployed or simulated
- The EOC can be activated
- Equipment and procedures identified in the emergency plan can be used
- Linkages with other organizations and agencies can be included
- Debriefing sessions should be included at the end of the exercise
- Lessons learned should be documented

Typical exercise types include the following:

- *Tabletop exercise*: A method of exercising plans in which participants review and discuss the actions they would take in response to a specific scenario, as presented by a facilitator. Specific actions are not performed.
- *Functional exercise*: A method of exercising plans in which participants perform some or all of the actions they would take in the event of plan activation to respond to a specific scenario.
- *Full operational exercise*: A method of exercising plans in which the participants suspend normal operation and activate the plans as if the event were real.

Response

The purpose of various incident management teams is to address critical incident response and recovery. A *critical incident* is defined as a sudden, unplanned event that affects or potentially affects corporate ability to execute critical business functions for some predetermined period of time and results in great damage or loss. Specifically, a critical incident interrupts normal business operations, requires an immediate coordinated response by numerous resources, and has the potential to focus extensive news media and public attention on the organization. The goals of the BCP are to protect human life, protect company assets and the surrounding community, contain the incident, communicate to all stakeholders (including the media), assess the effects of the critical incident correctly, and decide on and implement optimal response plans.

Important Crisis Management Skills

- *Be calm*: Crisis management requires clear thinking, emotional control, and balance.
- *Be open-minded*: Take in large quantities of information without tunnel vision, and focus on listening.
- *Be decisive*: Decisiveness needs to be balanced with a willingness to consider ideas and input from others. Be willing to prioritize and make decisions with only partial knowledge.
- *Be flexible*: Adapt to rapidly changing situations. Remember that some information relayed about critical incidents is incorrect or incomplete.
- *Be persuasive*: Crisis management requires the ability to convince others to follow directions.

Notification Levels

Regardless of the level of an incident, the IMT Lead (or his or her designate) notifies the CMT Lead of an emerging critical incident. Based on the incident's severity, the CMT Lead or designate determines when it is appropriate to communicate to respective CMT members at one of the three levels that is shown in Figure 6.3.

Information Level

- The CMT Lead is contacted by the IMT Lead regarding the incident. The CMT Lead contacts the remaining CMT members regarding the critical incident on a convenient basis, usually during working hours. The incident does not require a call to action.
- The IMT meets in order to manage the incident. The IMT Lead is responsible for tracking the incident status and updating the CMT Lead as necessary, who in turn updates the other CMT members accordingly.

If the incident is at a local level and is impacting people, assets, or brands, the LRT Lead is responsible for alerting the IMT Lead.

Alert Level

- The CMT Lead is contacted by the IMT Lead regarding the incident. The CMT Lead contacts the remaining CMT members regarding the critical incident regardless of the time of day.
- The CMT Lead contacts the other CMT Members to establish representation and availability in the event that the situation escalates and a meeting is required.

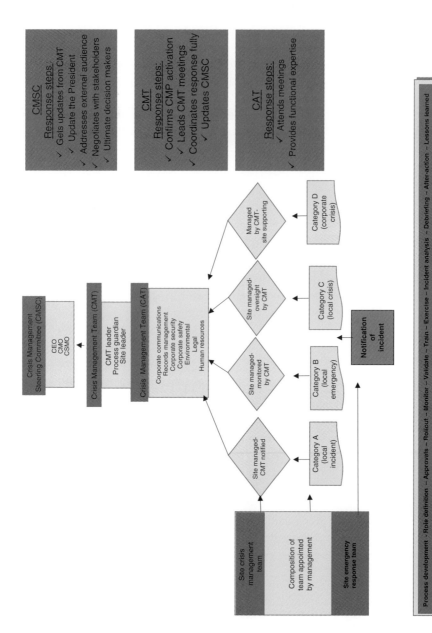

CMSC
Response steps:
✓ Gets updates from CMT
✓ Update the President
✓ Addresses external audience
✓ Negotiates with stakeholders
✓ Ultimate decision makers

CMT
Response steps:
✓ Confirms CMP activation
✓ Leads CMT meetings
✓ Coordinates response fully
  ✓ Updates CMSC

CAT
Response steps:
✓ Attends meetings
✓ Provides functional expertise

Crisis Management Steering Committee (CMSC)
CEO
CMO
CSMO

Crisis Management Team (CMT)
CMT leader
Process guardian
Site leader

Crisis Management Team (CAT)
Corporate communications
Records management
Corporate security
Corporate safety
Environmental
Legal
Human resources

Managed by CMT-
site supporting

Site managed-
oversight
by CMT

Site managed-
monitored
by CMT

Site managed-
CMT notified

Category D
(corporate
crisis)

Category C
(local crisis)

Category B
(local
emergency)

Category A
(local
incident)

Notification
of
incident

Site crisis
management
team

Composition of
team appointed
by management

Site emergency
response team

Process development – Role definition – Approvals – Rollout – Monitor – Validate – Train – Exercise – Incident analysis – Debriefing – After-action – Lessons learned

Figure 6.3 Incident notification flowchart.

- Additional key internal and external stakeholders are identified and placed on call if the situation escalates.
- The IMT meets in order to manage the incident from the corporate office level. The IMT Lead is responsible for tracking the incident status and updating the CMT Lead as necessary, who in turn updates the other CMT members accordingly.

If the incident is at a local level impacting people, assets, or brands, the LRT Lead is responsible for alerting the IMT Lead.

Immediate Level

- The CMT Lead is contacted by the IMT Lead regarding the incident. The CMT Lead contacts the remaining CMT members regarding the critical incident regardless of the time of day.
- The CMT Lead contacts the other CMT Members to establish representation and availability.
- Upon activation, respective CMT members will meet at a pre-designated site, as discussed in the "Crisis Management Meeting Locations" location.
- The IMT meets in order to manage the incident from the corporate office level. The IMT Lead is responsible for tracking the incident status and updating the CMT Lead as necessary, who in turn updates the other CMT members accordingly.

If the incident is at a local level and is impacting people, assets, or brands, the LRT Lead is responsible for alerting the IMT Lead; the LRT then meets.

Crisis Management Meeting Locations

The CMT, IMT, and LRT should have clearly defined meeting locations at the time of the emergency in which to meet and manage an incident accordingly. Some basic requirements of a primary and secondary meeting location should be as follows: they are equidistant, opposite directions of the corporate office or key facility in the event that the crisis involves the corporate office or key facility; there are sufficient tables, chairs, and meeting supplies for the team members to utilize; an extra copy of the BCP is secured there; there is ample parking; the site has redundant power, internet, TV, and telephone capability; and the site is accessible 24/7.

An EOC is a specific room or facility staffed by personnel charged with commanding, controlling, and coordinating the use of resources and personnel in response to a crisis. This room may be located at the corporate office. The EOC may be utilized 24/7 to monitor emerging risks such as weather and then fully utilized to support the management of a crisis. The EOC should have similar features to the other crisis management meeting locations mentioned in this chapter.

Recovery

Once the processes to be restored have been prioritized, the resumption work can begin, with processes restored according to the established prioritization schedule. The resumption of these processes may occur at either the current worksite or an alternate worksite, depending on the circumstances of the crisis. Documentation should be kept regarding when the processes are resumed. A facility property damage checklist is an effective tool to utilize in order to provide documentation of the damage suffered and how recovery should be prioritized. Once the critical processes have been resumed, resumption of the remaining processes can be addressed. Where possible, decisions about the prioritization of these processes should be thoroughly documented in advance, as should the timing of actual resumption.

Post-Incident Recovery and Record Keeping

Employees are encouraged to follow these instructions once authorities have reported that the area is safe and it has been cleared by local authorities. If possible, obtain written evidence of this authorization from the public authority.

First, Facility Management should attempt to secure the site. If it is not possible to complete this task alone, contact senior management and use your best judgment.

If the site cannot be secured, consult with management regarding the removal of high-value items from the site. Complete the facility property damage checklist. Take detailed notes on all damage, and take photographs, if possible. Detailed notes on all damaged assets include recording the item description, item number, and quantity. Be realistic when estimating quantities.

All equipment must be tested before use. If equipment needs repair, contact approved vendors for the specific equipment. Keep accurate records for hours spent by employees and outside vendors for clean-up or emergency repairs. Also, keep receipts for any expenses incurred for emergency repairs or replacement, or for expedient replenishment of equipment, inventory, and so on.

Accurate records as to when sites are closed by day and number of business hours, including financial information on lost revenues and any continued expenses during the shut-down period, are another area of critical record keeping. Coordinate with the appropriate retail management representatives prior to reopening stores. Note the date and time that the site reopened, together with the site's normal business hours. Also, report any public or governmental order affecting site operation. Additional reports on the activity of other businesses in the vicinity, or any unusual activity or extraordinary conditions occurring in the vicinity, should be recorded for future claims.

Each organization will need incident report forms for use following any incident. Attach additional pages of documentation with the incident report form, if necessary. Collect the completed incident report form along with all documentation from each impacted business unit.

Return to Normal Operations

The organization should seek to bring the company "back to normal" as quickly as is safe and reasonable. If it is not possible to return to the pre-crisis "normal," a "new normal" should be established. This "new normal" creates the expectation that, while there may be changes and restructuring in the workplace, the organization will phase back into productive work. Each step of the process and all decisions should be carefully documented. Coordination with senior management on timing for these "normal" or "new normal" decisions is required.

As a rule, it is at this point that the crisis may be officially declared over. Again, it is important to document this decision. Press conferences and mass media communications may be undertaken to bolster employee and client confidence.

Corrective Action Plan

A corrective action plan is a process that follows an actual occurrence or exercise to identify program shortfalls and necessary corrective actions to address those shortfalls. The corrective action plan provides the techniques to manage the capabilities improvement process.

The corrective action plan generally begins following the "after-action" discussion or critique of the incident or exercise. The corrective action plan can also begin during the incident if a lengthy or extended event is being managed. During the evaluation, process deficiencies that require improvement are noted. Some corrective actions might not be taken immediately because of constraints, such as budgets, staffing, or contracts, and might be deferred as a part of a long-range project. However, temporary actions should be taken to implement the desired option.

Typically, deficiencies fall within one or more of the program elements covered by this standard. There are three categories: plan or standard operating procedures (SOP) revisions, training, and equipment additions or modifications and facilities. The following should be addressed in the corrective action plan:

- State the problem, and identify its impact.
- Review the history of corrective action issues, and identify solutions.
- Select a corrective action strategy, and prioritize the actions to be taken as well as an associated timeline for completion.
- Provide authority and resources to the individual assigned to implementation so that the designated change can be accomplished.
- Identify the resources required to implement the strategy.
- Check on the progress for completing the corrective action.
- Forward problems that need to be resolved by higher authorities to the level of authority that can.

Summary and Conclusions

The BCP offered in this chapter provides a detailed blueprint for an entire cycle of plans, training, and assessment of plans and preparedness tools that are essential for any business enterprise to adopt as the FM department readies the organization for the unknown and unexpected. With these plans, the unexpected becomes expected and the unknown becomes known. The advantage of adopting a corporate BCP is to be prepared as much as possible for a disaster so that once it happens, the organization can follow the developed blueprint and utilize its training experience to best handle the business enterprise during the crisis, in addition to any public emergency assistance to restore operations. The BCP provides the organization with the skills, mind-set, and action steps to handle disaster. This is one function that focuses FM preparedness on its ability to make the difference between business continuity and business collapse.

Changing Workplaces and Distributed Work

Kathy O. Roper

Georgia Institute of Technology, Atlanta, GA

The world of work has changed dramatically over the last two decades. The creation of facility management (FM) as a separate profession had its start in the 1970s corporate worlds of personal computing, open landscape furniture development, and new management trends that recognized personal differences in workers and began to adjust and adopt new measures of performance management. Since that time, increasing advances in information and communications technology (ICT) have enabled a more mobile workforce, and the concept of Knowledge Age workers who provide information and services rather than "widgets" that can be easily counted or measured has led to a dramatic change in the workplace itself, and to new ways of working that individuals expect today and in the near future.

This chapter will provide a brief overview of the dramatic change to Knowledge Age work, a look at some of the issues associated with these changes, the rise of distributed work, the impacts to FM, and some suggestions for improved support through well-designed and well-managed workplaces. The whole concept of "workplace" has changed, and workers no longer expect that "the workplace" will be only the centrally located, grand office complex housing workers on regular schedules or with fully assigned offices that they "own" during their tenure with an organization.

The Knowledge Age

Since the dawn of humankind, people needed knowledge to survive everyday life. Early humans lived in communities where there was no formal education, and individuals independently or in small groups

---

International Facility Management, First Edition. Kathy O. Roper and Lisa J. Borello.
© 2014 John Wiley & Sons, Ltd. Published 2014 by John Wiley & Sons, Ltd.

decided how they would prioritize their work and productivity. If farmers wanted to grow enough for only their family, then that was possible. Others, however, decided to grow more than what was needed for their family and trade with others for baskets, pottery, or other needs. The use of animals and/or humans was required to grow crops and hunt to survive. Muscle power was the dominate means of productivity in the Agrarian Age.

In the mid-nineteenth century, the invention of all types of mechanical aids to improve or replace muscle power with mechanical power ushered in the Industrial Age. Instead of human planters and animals pulling plows, machinery replaced these functions. Humans became more efficient, but a new kind of knowledge was needed to understand the complexities of building and operating the machinery. Schools developed and rapidly expanded, providing populations with dramatically different lifestyles as parents no longer provided all of the education the children of the society needed. The mechanical power replacing the dominant muscle power required that new concepts be developed to manage these Industrial Age improvements. "Management" as a new occupation took hold, was taught in schools, and advanced mechanical concepts toward more and more efficiency.

Later in the Industrial Age, around the early twentieth century, efficiency extended to take precedence over the needs of humans. A one-size-fits-all system seemed to work well as a way of sorting machines and even people into the different categories for improved efficiency. However, this drive toward greater and great productivity reached extremes with humans, who have limits in their physical ability to maximize efficiency. In other words, the human "machine" could be pushed only so far. The development of unions, regulations to protect workers, and social change ensued. Additional mechanical developments led to the creation of computing in the mid-twentieth century.

The advent of computers led the way for the "post-industrial" or Knowledge Age that is now fully developing at the start of the twenty-first century. People now need new and additional kinds of knowledge. The trend requires people to be able to do things with this knowledge, and to use knowledge itself to create additional knowledge. Knowledge and brain power have now become the dominate resources, outstripping Industrial Age mechanization as the primary value in society.

Instead of primary work in manufacturing plants and factories, workers moved into office settings to assemble concepts and document processes and ideas that together launched new ways of work. At the same time, the development of computing was moving manual paperwork in the direction of what we now know as digital information. Rather than manual or mechanical labor, workers use their knowledge, personal connections, and specialized or widely available information to improve products and services, or to create new commercial opportunities. Rather than paperwork, workers perform knowledge work.

Knowledge Age workers and citizens of today's societies need to be able to find, assess, and represent new information rapidly. They need to be able to communicate with others, to work productively in collaborations with others, and to assemble diverse concepts to produce new information.

Knowledge Age skills include adaptability, creativity, and innovativeness. A dramatic change is that these knowledge workers need to be able to think and learn for themselves. Sometimes help may come in the form of external authorities, systems, or rules, but frequently knowledge workers are on their own without help or direction from others. This impacts educational needs, but our schools are changing slowly and not providing the rapid development seen in the marketplace. Management theories developed during the Industrial Age are slowing incorporating knowledge into the mix to provide new tools for human innovation management. With a lack of fully developed theories and processes either in the workplace or taught in higher education for knowledge work, the responsibility for adaptability is on individual workers once they leave school and enter the marketplace.

Knowledge Age workers are quickly evolving from Industrial Age education and training platforms to migrate into new ways of working collaboratively and across time and distances, even if they often must do this without support from traditional educational or societal means. Change has become a given, and adaptability to change is demanded. Successful workers are those who observe their surroundings, orient themselves toward new developments and trends, take charge of deciding on what strategy to utilize to move ahead and improve their productivity, and finally take action based on the prior cycle of "observe, orient, decide, and act" (OODA), which was developed in the US Air Force by Colonel John Boyd (Watson, 2007). Boyd's cycle, as it is often called, has been used in many situations to help provide a context for change and improvement.

Distributed Work

With advances in ICT, the ability for everyone to have ubiquitous connectivity (whether via the Internet or phone) has allowed workers to change the settings they utilize for work and therefore change what is required for workplaces. Workers find that they are now able to truly work anytime, anyplace. These changes occur organically as individuals upgrade their devices and knowledge of their use. For the most part, individuals today are far more advanced than their organization's policies regarding anytime, anyplace working. First, let us define distributed work and then provide examples of how distributed work settings can be used successfully.

Distributed work is a collection of options for workers, especially knowledge workers, to enable them to individually select not only how they produce but also, in many cases, what they produce. Enabled through the Internet, secured data exchange, and inexpensive devices to connect to information at any time, these knowledge workers are self-managed and often work out the details of how to collaborate without oversight or supervision.

Knowledge workers understand best what they need to be productive, and they make sure the devices, connectivity, and collaboration are in place. This new self-management concept is also dramatically altering the way that work is conducted in major organizations across the world.

The dramatic change in organizations and workers is driven by a number of broad issues. Figure 7.1 shows some of the major issues that promote distributed workplaces as the new way of working for knowledge work today. Economics is always at the forefront of business change, driving down costs and spending within the organization. New regulations and a global focus on environmental issues such as greenhouse gas reduction, alternative energy possibilities, and carbon emission reporting requirements also force organizations to consider how workers assemble if face-to-face work is not required.

Knowledge workers today in most advanced economies are also driving change as they demand greater flexibility to fulfill family obligations along with work responsibilities. Technology has advanced to the point where this is now possible. With this ability in place, workers

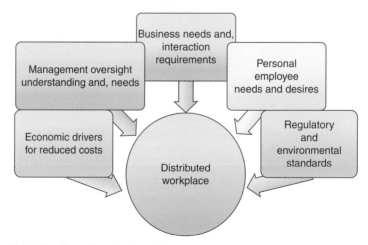

Figure 7.1   Distributed workplace drivers.

are now demanding flexibility; and with the aging populations in many advanced countries, the ability to attract and retain key talent is very high on organizations' list of requirements in the Knowledge Age. If workers can work more flexibly in another organization, they may be lost, so senior management is recognizing the value that workplace diversity and flexibility can bring to their competitive advantage.

Perhaps the lagging drivers of distributed workplace accommodations are the business and management needs within the organization. As mentioned in this chapter, the educational system, especially in management and business, has lagged behind on many of the "human factors" that impact leadership and management skills. Many organizations' managers still struggle with productivity metrics for knowledge workers when their education provided only financial return on investment styles of analysis. How do they now validate engagement and increases for knowledge workers who are more satisfied, creative, innovative, and productive? What do they count: new ideas per hour? The move away from "widget counting" to coaching and motivating knowledge workers is subtle and yet dramatically different from older management styles. FM can provide assistance here with user satisfaction measures, absenteeism and utilization metrics, as well as provision of new office designs that provide the needed collaboration *and* focused workspaces that knowledge workers need.

What Are Distributed Workplaces?

Distributed workplaces typically include a number of new types of work spaces, as offices planners and designers have learned what knowledge workers need and prefer. The "open-office" design was the first step toward providing a more collaborative space for workers. Cubicles were assigned to workers often based on hierarchy rather than function. Entry-level employees received small cubes, middle management was given medium cubes, and executive management may still reside in large enclosed offices, typically on top floors providing nice views. This hierarchy system led to higher costs for the provision of facilities since any organizational change elevating workers to higher levels required space changes to match hierarchy demands. Not only were the building costs high, but also downtime to rebuild and loss of productivity are generally overlooked.

Newer office designs have moved away from enclosed offices, providing most employees with cubicle spaces that are either assigned or as needed. This flexibility to move from space to space throughout the day, as function rather than assignment dictate, is the newest trend and provides multiple options for workers to choose what suits them best at any time. These new concepts include "benching" and fully mobile or virtual working.

Benching is an office design concept that furthers the collaborative elements of cubicles by removing the cubicle panels, and has workers sitting side by side and face to face as if sharing a "bench." The work surfaces may or may not include separations, allowing workers to float across whatever space is needed. These benching areas can be used for primary work or project spaces. They also work well for drop-in workers as "touchdown" spaces for short-term use while in the office (Aznavoorian and Doherty, 2011). Benching has been adopted in many high-technology companies as a means of reducing space, bringing workers together to enable collaborative efforts, as well as providing one of the multiple spaces that workers might need for knowledge work in distributed settings.

Virtual work is normally defined as complete independence on assigned space for a worker. Independent contractors are obvious examples of successful fully mobile work. These workers use ICT to contact clients, collaborators, vendors, and regulators anytime and from any place. They may have home offices, or they might utilize shared executive suites when meetings and other "office" settings are needed. They do not have one workplace but many. The classic example of successful virtual work is the salesperson who makes client calls from the car and visits clients in their offices or at restaurants, golf courses, and event facilities. Such employees may provide reports to their home office via email or direct links via the Internet from any number of current devices (e.g. iPads, smart phones, and traditional personal computers), and they may have extremely flexible working schedules to accommodate client entertaining during the evening and weekends, as well as meeting routine business meeting requirements during the work week. Students are another example of virtual knowledge workers since their work is distributed across classrooms, dorm rooms, libraries, and other collaborative spaces of their own choosing. Virtual workers are independent workers, whether they have a management structure in which they report or are self-employed.

One key aspect of knowledge work is the ability to interact and communicate with others to share and advance knowledge. This type of collaborative space is being designed to draw in workers and maintain their connectivity to ICT as they move around the office space. Lounge-style seating with mobility is often the preferred choice for these spaces, along with some tables and, again, movable equipment, so that workers can adapt what they need without having to wait for meeting rooms to become available, or submit work requests to have furniture moved. The workers quickly pull mobile tables from workstations to conferencing areas and instantly have project meetings with wi-fi connectivity or easy access to the needed databases and libraries of information they need.

But these workers also need quiet spaces to gather, read, and process information, or reassemble and draft the new knowledge they are developing. This is why innovative organizations have learned that distributed workplaces are not necessarily smaller in proportion to the flexibility of the space, since multiple spaces are required. However, the workers also do not "own" specific spaces in most distributed workplace designs, so there are trade-offs between multiple locations for knowledge workers throughout the day. Currently, however, it seems that distributed work arrangements are still primarily being utilized by outsourced workers and accounting, IT, and sales personnel rather than the broader knowledge worker (International Facility Management Association [IFMA], 2009). Management concern about disrupting staff expectations in changing from old-style individual offices or cubicle provisions to more innovative shared, distributed spaces has limited acceptance.

Management Issues in Distributed Work

It should be recognized that regardless of whether management approves, knowledge workers are already working in distributed ways. They still may be required to come to a centralized main office, but they meet with colleagues in coffee shops, restaurants, and break rooms. They text and tweet their collaborators for instant discussion of ideas, and they may possibly work from home on detailed, head-down types of work in order to reduce the interruptions normally encountered in the workplace. So organizations should recognize this and maximize the efficiency possible from these new ways of working.

Distributed workplaces have been available for many years, but the advances in communications technology and its security have recently made the dramatic change in workers' ability to work anywhere possible. Management is still catching up and is seen today as the largest barrier in many organizations to more acceptance of distributed work.

There are progressive organizations that have learned how to measure knowledge work, and they are empowering their knowledge workers to understand and utilize their personalized ways of working to maximize productivity. Limiting workers to specific times and places certainly cannot maximize each individual worker's preferences for productive work. Some of us are morning people, preferring to immediately produce early in the day, while others need time to rise before they shine, so to speak. Requiring productivity from them at 8:00 a.m. could result in reduced productivity as well as lack of engagement with the organization overall, since they do not feel respected or trusted to provide the needed production on their own schedule. Although this may not be possible for all workers, knowledge workers generally have flexibility to provide input to reports, share ideas, and develop their work potentially at all hours of the day. Perhaps someone is prone to discover innovations in the middle of the night after awakening from dreams providing insight. She may rise and document some of her ideas at 3:00 a.m., allowing maximum productivity for her individualized preferences. Personalization and flexibility are key issues that motivate and aid knowledge workers. Managers need to recognize this more by evaluating output rather than hours in the main office. Facility managers cannot dictate management policies, but they can certainly provide the facility tools to support the flexibility and personalization needed to help workers maximize productivity in the workplace setting.

Additional issues in modern workplaces include diversity issues for cultures and generations, as well as new issues regarding social responsibility in the organizational setting. The remainder of this section will provide a short overview of each of these important transitions in considering distributed workplaces within an organization. All sub-sections incorporate concepts that have been mentioned in this chapter, but will also uncover unique attributes.

Cultural Diversity

Diversity of cultures has been in the workplace for many years, but ease of travel, relaxed work regulations in some countries, and developing education have caused a more diverse mix of cultures across all countries. Workplace accommodation of these cultural issues avoids problems that can sap productivity, and it keeps workers engaged and moving productively in the workplace. Cultural diversity in the work-place has been the responsibility of human resource organizations, who develop and apply policies that encourage diversity and avoid issues when diverse cultures are in the workplace. But FM has responsibilities here, too. A program to recognize and address issues might include reli-gious issues, such as by providing restrooms that meet specific religious needs, areas for those who worship throughout the day, or possibly consideration of food issues in company snack machines and cafeterias.

Multinational organizations with facilities in diverse locations through-out the world have dealt with these issues and have guidelines that could benefit cross-border companies who are new to cultural diversity. It is also critical for facility managers in new countries to utilize local experts to avoid any mistakes in providing or not providing needed designs or services based on local culture. Workplaces that can encourage tolerance and understanding of many cultures are successful in accommodating multicultural workforces. A number of case examples are available in the 2011 *Work on the Move* book from the International Facility Management Association (IFMA) Foundation (Coles, 2011).

Generational Diversity

A new concept in mature societies is the realization that fully four generations of workers are remaining in today's workforce. For various reasons, including healthier aging, reduced retirement income due to global financial issues, and the need for many organizations to retain aging workers due to smaller generations to provide new workers, the workforce has become generationally diverse. The needs of older workers are different from those of young workers. Physical issues may concern older workers needing accommodations in the workplace to remain comfortable and productive. Technology issues provide the opportunity for younger workers to expect "student lifestyles" in their new work settings. Understanding and providing for the four generations are new expectations for facility provisioning. Close ties to human resource organizations can provide more details on the needs of the individual generations, but overall, the growth of diversity in workers must be accommodated by facility organizations worldwide.

Social Responsibility

Energy conservation issues have long been topics of importance in FM, but additional corporate concerns with clean air, transportation, indoor environmental quality, lighting, and building and facility materials all contribute to how users and customers view our organizations. Sustainability initiatives are worldwide and growing. Not only are benefits accruing to organizations that choose green buildings, but also increasing regulations in many parts of the world may soon dictate compliance with many environmental and social regulations.

One strong new option is the Global Reporting Initiative (GRI), which focuses corporate gathering of standardized metrics on social and environmental issues in addition to financial measures. Through transparent reporting, the GRI mission states,

A sustainable global economy should combine long term profitability with social justice and environmental care. This means that, for organizations, sustainability covers the key areas of economic, environmental, social and governance performance. (GRI, 2013)

Other concepts such as the "triple bottom line," which is reporting on environmental protection and social equity in addition to economic success, was first developed in 1994 by John Elkington in *Cannibals with Forks* (Elkington, 1994). The title, taken from a Polish poet who asked, "Is it progress if a cannibal uses a fork?" provides the broad setting for change in a corporate agenda focused solely on financial success, often at the expense of social and environmental concerns. Although the concepts of social responsibility are filtering into business, the profit initiative is still the strongest motivator, and facility professionals must become better acquainted with financial measures in order to help promote and affect change toward the triple bottom line of people, planet, and profit in our facilities.

Preparing for the future is wise, but organizations are seeing multiple benefits from lower operating costs, attracting and retaining top talent, and gaining marketing benefits from consumers by becoming a company with sustainable facilities. Additional positive impacts to improve employee health, productivity, and individual control of temperature, lighting, noise, and other building elements provide tremendous benefits overall. These include increased worker engagement, loyalty, and productivity.

Successful Distributed Workplaces

A number of forward-thinking organizations have begun implementing distributed workplace settings and designs for their knowledge workers. Among them are many of the high-tech companies one would expect to be early adopters of innovative workplaces. Key among the successful concepts is the development of an overall workplace strategy within the organization. This strategy will help to define and provide the best solution for each individual organization.

Steps to Developing Successful Distributed Workplace Strategies

The first step in any planning process is to understand current conditions and align goals with the business imperatives of the organization. Initial research on distributed workplace arrangements has shown that business-driven initiatives hold a much stronger success rate and higher user buy-in and acceptance than those projects that are driven by cost reduction only (Becker and Steele, 1995). Business-driven motivations might include increases in worker productivity, support for teaming and collaboration, aligning processes with space design, and other reasons that motivate workers.

The second step includes the development of the strategy team and resources to support the process. The development of a distributed workplace strategy could be seen as a planning project. As with any project, clear definitions of resources and boundaries for the project help to clarify the project and speed implementation once plans are agreed and approved.

A logical third step in distributed workplace strategy development is the identification of categories of space and the interaction of players in each category. The delineation of work roles is needed to identify those who benefit from specific strategies. A one-for-all format is not usually successful since different functional roles dictate different work strategies. Issues to be considered in this step include worker requirements for contacts, the type of work, the frequency of each type, and the complexity of the work. A worker with high interaction rates and high work complexity may need extremes in both collaborative and focused workspace options. Another worker with low-complexity tasks and few interactions may focus primarily in virtual and noncollaborative spaces, for example.

Next, the distributed workplace strategy should address the needs of the workers in comparison to the existing conditions. This gap in provisioning will provide the overall scope of change required. A recommendation with potential alternatives would be next, followed by approvals to fund and change according to the new distributed workplace strategy. Buy-in by both user groups and senior management is key to successful implementation of any major change.

Finally, the actual project to realign the space to meet the new strategy will begin. This final implementation stage should also include education and training for the workers so that they can manage the workplace changes successfully. Often, a "sales" approach is needed to give users positive information on why and how the distributed workplace strategy is important. Change is difficult and rarely welcomed by humans, so addressing this process is also a critical element of implementation. Formal change management processes have been used successfully in organizations by either hiring experts for this role or having FM professionals provide the process. With ongoing change in the workplace, change management is a new skill required for FM professionals.

Examples of Success

An often cited example of successful distributed workplace arrangements is Cisco Systems, the multinational consumer electronics and networking company. As a provider of network connectivity across many platforms and locations, Cisco was an early adopter of distributed workplace arrangements, and its corporate headquarters in San Jose, California, demonstrates a number of typical strategies. The early findings for Cisco included higher levels of employee satisfaction with the technologies, light, openness, and improved collaboration opportunities; and savings of between 37 and 60% for rent, construction furniture, and other workplace costs. However, many workers who had spent most of their time at assigned workstations were more challenged by the new distributed working styles (Heerwagen, Kelly, and Kampschroer, 2010).

These can be important lessons from early adopters, and they point to areas on which to focus more attention for our projects.

Another example comes from Madrid's Kellogg Company headquarters project. This new headquarters project provided Kellogg with the opportunity to reinforce work changes with changes toward a more distributed workplace design and ways to reinforce the need for collaborative work. Their slogan for the new space, "Work is what we do, not where we go," reinforced the theme; this approach garnered savings in facility costs to support personnel, modified spaces for organizational changes, and reduced energy costs, and the attraction of new employees has been significantly improved through social benefits that appear to be more important than salary for some employees (North, 2011).

Measurements for benefits from distributed workplace strategies can also be hard to document. One example can be found by Sven Govaars of Gensler:

> For a population of 1,000 people, with 25 percent employee participation, a projected two percent increase in productivity, retention of 3.5 percent (industry norm) and gaining one additional hour of work a day, the savings year over year was upward of $1 million. For a capital expenditure of $10 million, the offset benefit over 10 years would drive the cost near zero. (Govaars, 2012)

Similar calculations can be found, showing that the conversion of personnel time into average salaries can reap substantial savings for even small increases in productivity. Giving employees more time to focus and reducing interruptions can dramatically improve productivity and increase competitive advantage for those organizations providing distributed ways of working for knowledge workers.

Summary and Conclusions

The workforce is changing, utilizing advanced ICT with personal devices and altering their own work schedules to meet work–life balance challenges, with or without organizational authorization. The benefits that FM professionals can realize by capturing these changes in the workplace can dramatically change the workplace itself and allow for savings in space, utilities, furniture, and fixtures, as well as provide motivation for increased productivity of workers, thus tremendously benefitting the bottom line of the organization. If workers are happier, productivity is increased, social and environmental impacts are improved, and competitive advantages are bound to be realized. This is already the new way of working, and it will become more expected in the near future; facility management must be onboard.

References

Aznavoorian, L., and Doherty, P. (2011). Evolution of the workplace. In *Work on the move driving strategy and change in workplaces*. Houston, TX: IFMA Foundation, p. 43.

Becker, F., and Steele, F. (1995). *Workplace by design: mapping the high-performance workscape*. San Francisco: Jossey-Bass.

Coles, D. (Ed.). (2011). *Work on the move: driving strategy and change in the workplace*. Houston, TX: IFMA Foundation.

Elkington, J. (1994). *Cannibals with forks*. New York: John Wiley & Sons, Inc.

Global Reporting Initiative (GRI). 2013. About GRI. Available at: https://www.globalreporting.org/Information/about-gri/Pages/default.aspx (accessed 22 January 2013).

Govaars, S. (2012). Measuring workplace benefits: using intuition in an evidence-based world. *The Leader*, November–December, p. 30.

Heerwagen, J., Kelly, K., and Kampschroer, K. (2010). The changing nature of organizations, work, and workplace. In *Whole building design guide*. Available at: http://www.wbdg.org/resources/chngorgwork.php (accessed 20 December 2012).

International Facility Management Association (IFMA). (2009). *Distributed work research report no. 31*. Houston, TX: IFMA.

North, K. (2011). Case studies from around the world. In *Work on the move: driving strategy and change in the workplace*. Houston, TX: IFMA Foundation, p. 185.

Watson, G.H. (2007). *Strategic Benchmarking Reloaded with Six Sigma*. Hoboken, NJ: John Wiley & Sons, Inc.

Measuring Work

Matthew Tucker

Liverpool John Moores University, Liverpool, UK

Introduction: Why Measure Performance?

Facility managers have a responsibility to effectively manage buildings and infrastructure to optimise the ability of the people and/or businesses to use them to meet their core objectives. Facility management (FM) providers will do this over a given contractual period, to which they are judged on their level of success in handling such operations. Hence, the way in which facility managers measure the performance of their operations is crucial, to prove their business worth. To that end, it is important to understand what we mean by performance measurement, and how this relates to FM.

Performance measurement is concerned with the process of collecting and analysing related data that will help measure predetermined goals in order to understand the level or extent to which these goals have been achieved and, further, how these goals can be improved. Performance measurement is a critical instrument in determining the continual improvement of facility operations. Neely (1999) established seven main reasons for the emergence of performance measurement:

- *The changing nature of work*: reduction in labour and rise of automation
- *Increasing competition*: reducing cost whilst still achieving best value
- *Specific improvement initiatives*: introduction of quality management systems
- *National and international awards*: added pressure to prove performance

International Facility Management, First Edition. Kathy O. Roper and Lisa J. Borello.
© 2014 John Wiley & Sons, Ltd. Published 2014 by John Wiley & Sons, Ltd.

- *Changing organisational roles*: shifting focus from outputs to processes and structures
- *Changing external demands*: increasing need to provide evidence to meet performance standards
- *The power of information technology*: constantly evolving and creating new opportunities.

Furthermore, Kaplan and Norton (1996) emphasise the need to acquire information, aptly stating that 'companies are in the midst of a revolutionary transformation. Industrial age competition is shifting to information age competition'. Kaplan and Norton (1996) agree, however, that this has had a much greater impact on the service sector, as service industries previously existed in relatively uncompetitive environments.

However, one would contend that we have now outlived this 'information age competition' as companies are now in the midst of a more profound revolutionary transformation, shifting from information age competition to social age competition. We now live in the social age, where we have moved beyond the information age of fast and fluent data transfer, collection and inputting to a more profound level of doing such things within a closely connected global social network that has the ability to immediately judge and opine the outcomes of such capturing of information.

Performance measurement is a major business mechanism, enabling organisational change, improvement and future superiority. This chapter provides the background and context to some of the overarching theories and concepts of performance measurement, then focuses on how this is applied within FM and, finally, looks ahead at some of the drivers and challenges that FM will need to grapple with in the near future.

Foundations of Performance Measurement

Setting a Benchmark Standard

A critical component of FM is the ability to benchmark the performance of facility operations against others. However, the concept of benchmarking is often not fully appreciated, and it can be mistreated within the field of FM. Camp (1989) provided one of the first studies on performance measurement theory, based on his research on and experience benchmarking at Xerox, which is generally accepted as the first company to kick-start the effective application of benchmarking performance measurement (McDougall and Hinks, 2000; Massheder and Finch, 1998b) within the West, with Japan being the nation to originate the theory (Zairi, 1994). For Camp, benchmarking is not about just incorporating the best and taking the strengths of those in your competitive circle, but to emulate them and then go further by installing your own best practice to reach a superior position in the market.

To summarise this,

Camp identifies four basic steps that are fundamental to benchmarking success:

- *Know your operation*: Evaluate internal operation strengths and weaknesses.
- *Know the industry leaders or competitors*: Know the strengths and weaknesses of the competition.
- *Incorporate the best*: Emulate the strengths of the leaders in competition.
- *Gain superiority*: Go beyond the best practices installed, and be the best of the best.

Camp contends that benchmarking is split into two elements: practices and metrics. Practices are the methods used (i.e. the process), and metrics are the quantified effect of installing the practices (i.e. the output or measure). Camp's (1989) theory works from a gap-based process, where the practices are first investigated once they are understood they can be quantified to show their numeric effect.

Camp highlights that 'maturity' is achieved when the benchmarking processes become ongoing and are embedded into work practices. However, an important point to take into account within the benchmarking process is the fact that benchmarking is essentially a top-down activity (Zairi, 1994): although it encourages internal improvements (e.g. problem solving and employee empowerment), its core focus is to be used for objective setting by senior management, and its consequent deployment to the organisational teams (Zairi, 1994).

Transition from Core to Noncore Measures

A key factor that has changed the nature of how businesses measure performance is the dichotomy between the use of financial (quantitative) indicators and the lack of nonfinancial (qualitative) indicators. Traditionally, the use of financial indicators has dominated the way in which businesses measure their performance. With the considerable influence of social networks and the influence of peer-reviewing business performance, this philosophy is no longer sustainable, and the emergence of nonfinancial or qualitative indicators, specifically focused on process, structure and change instead of traditional cost, profit and output, has changed the way in which businesses perceive performance.

Varcoe (1996) contends that these traditional, or financial, measures are past their "sell by date" (p. 47). They are likely to be from "outdated standard costing systems which are primarily designed to satisfy external financial reporting purposes ... rather than the needs of continual improvement in internal operational performance" (p. 47). Varcoe uses as an example the requirement to "performance measure" budgets (1996). These types of measures are used to determine the cash flow and expenditure trends over the year in an attempt to 'drive overall expenditures down' (1996). However, what these measures do not achieve is addressing the overall value that is obtained from the expenditure; they seek only an accounting perspective focused on bringing down costs with no reflection assessing the overall quality of the outcome along the way.

From a benchmarking perspective, Zairi (1994) criticises why the West took so long to implement benchmarking theory as a key performance measurement technique, contending that a key reason was that managers have traditionally been trained to make decisions based on financial information. Zairi (1994) notes three shortcomings of financial information: (1) it lacks relevance to the process that delivers value to the end customer; (2) it is compiled historically, becoming irrelevant by the time decisions are actually made; and (3) methods used for measuring performance are not very compatible with modern business approaches.

Revolutionising Performance Measurement in the Service Sector

A study by Fitzgerald *et al.* (1991) was one of the first to highlight the complexity of measuring performance within the service sector, as opposed to that of the manufacturing sector. A distinction should be made between 'goods' and 'services', where services are primarily intangible. Fitzgerald *et al.* (1991) details this distinction more specifically, highlighting four differences, which are as follows:

- *Intangibility*: Unlike manufacturing, the service is likely to be focused on performances rather than objects, or a mixture of both.
- *Heterogeneous*: Service outputs are heterogeneous as their standard of performance may vary, making it hard to ensure constant quality.
- *Simultaneous*: Production and consumption of many services are simultaneous, so they cannot be counted, measured, inspected or tested in advance of sale for subsequent delivery to customer.
- *Perishability*: Services cannot be stored; therefore, the scheduling of operations and controlling quality are key management problems.

In light of these four characteristics, Fitzgerald *et al.* (1991) contend that it is necessary to measure across a range of variables. Traditionally, we have seen an overemphasis on financial or cost-orientated measures; when focusing on services in particular, this causes neglect and mismanagement of the more intangible nonfinancial measures. To this,

Fitzgerald *et al.* (1991) proposed some key generic dimensions to measure service performance, which included the following:

- *Quality*: reliability, responsiveness, aesthetics, cleanliness, comfort, friendliness, communication, courtesy, competence, access, availability and security
- *Flexibility*: volume flexibility, delivery speed flexibility and specification flexibility
- *Resource utilisation*: productivity and efficiency
- *Innovation*: performance of the innovation process and performance of individual innovations.

The Balanced Scorecard – the Strategic Performance Measurement System

Kaplan and Norton (1996) established arguably the most prominent performance measurement theory to date; it is the most influential and successful in the field of performance measurement (de Waal, 2003). Originating from Harvard Business School, Kaplan and Norton (1996) delivered a theory that can be embedded into long-term business strategy, making it sustainable and productive. Mirroring the views of Fitzgerald *et al.* (1991), Kaplan and Norton (1996) contend that the impact of the information age is more prominent and important for the service sector than for manufacturing. Kaplan and Norton (1996) feel that it has become more important to exploit intangible assets, which enable organisations to develop customer relationships, introduce innovative products and services, produce high-quality products and services, mobilise employment skills and motivation and deploy information technology systems.

To this end, Kaplan and Norton (1996) identified four key perspectives in which business performance measurement systems should operate:

- *Financial*: Objectives relate to profitability and indicate whether the company strategy is contributing to bottom-line improvement.
- *Customer*: Includes customer satisfaction, retention, acquisition, profitability, and market and account share in target segments
- *Internal business process*: Identifies the critical internal processes of the organisation that will have the greatest impact on customer satisfaction
- *Learning and growth*: Key part of the process to ensure future sustainability; focused on people, systems and organisational procedures.

The main function of the Balanced Scorecard essentially is to provide a framework for translating an organisation's vision into a key set of performance indicators that are structured around the four perspectives discussed here (Amaratunga and Baldry, 2000).

The main focus here is on long-term strategy – sustainable business improvement. Their theories are not merely for quick-win, short-term profitability, but to establish strategic business processes that will become embedded into company culture. Kaplan and Norton (1996) emphasise the need for businesses to have 'vision and strategy', by being able to retain short-term performance but clearly revealing value drivers for longer term competitive performance. The ability for FM to use such tools is not new; however, they are too often applied in an ad hoc manner without considering the full theoretical context behind them. This initial section has set out to provide the reader with a more thorough grounding of how FM can utilise the attributes of benchmarking across a balanced scorecard of key performance indicators (KPIs). The "Evolution of Performance Measurement in FM" section looks at how such techniques can be applied within FM.

Evolution of Performance Measurement in FM

Importance of Performance Measurement in FM

The contemporary challenge for FM companies is to deliver services that are faster, better and cheaper. The only way to prove whether an organisation is achieving this is through effective performance measurement. The need to reduce costs and simultaneously add value from services (Price and Akhlaghi, 1999) means that the convergence between performance measurement and FM is critical.

Amaratunga and Baldry (2002b) emphasise the strategic nature of performance measurement within organisations, stating that "for the economic health of the organisation, the senior management at the core of the business will want to know the performance of facilities" (p. 332). However, traditional performance measures tend to be narrowly focused on financial outputs, reflecting reluctance to look at a balanced scorecard approach. This has also tended to be the case within the FM industry.

A Balanced Scorecard in FM?

The FM industry has had a relatively recent development in comparison to its counterpart disciplines within the built environment, in which one could argue that the performance measurement processes in place within FM have been slow to evolve into more noncore performance measures. This is acknowledged by Amaratunga et al. (2000, 2001), who emphasise that traditional performance measurement systems in FM focus primarily on financial indicators, but this is no longer an adequate measure of competitiveness for contemporary performance measurement systems in the information era.

Jones and Sharp (2007) emphasise the need to align business needs with built-asset maintenance expenditure decisions. Jones and Sharp (2007) contend that expenditure decisions are based on the building alone, rather than considering the impact of the business within the building. Jones and Sharp (2007) state that "an obsolescence gap develops in which the building is unable to meet all the demands placed on it" (p. 526). Jones and Sharp (2007) go on to emphasise that "this obsolescence gap, and in particular the impact that it has on the performance of the activities that take place within the building, is what is critical to building owners/users, and not the condition of the building *per se*" (p. 526).

One could contend from this that measuring maintenance performance based on the needs of the organisation, rather than the building, will add value to the FM function and in turn to the organisation. Reiterating the views of Amaratunga *et al.* (2000), FM performance measurement needs to go beyond the narrow focus of the physical infrastructure and numerical measures, to a balance of measures that takes account of how FM can perform to improve the business processes of the organisation within a building. In essence, the focus of FM performance measurement is on the *organisation*, not the building, from a balanced set of indicators.

Despite the traditional cost-focused culture regarding performance measurement in FM, it is a crucial component in the achievement of strategic FM service delivery. Amaratunga *et al.* (2000) acknowledge this, saying that "performance measurement is really at the heart of good FM practice". They go on to link this importance within the context of developing an FM strategy, where in order for organisations to translate their business objectives into current and future FM needs, they will also want to "maximise the performance of its facilities, balancing business needs with cost" (Amaratunga *et al.*, 2000). Moreover, Tranfield and Akhlaghi (1995) consider the importance of FM performance within the context of change, which raises many questions, including:

- Are we doing the right things?
- How well or otherwise do we perform?
- How do we compare with others within our industry and outside it?
- How can we improve our performance?

In addition to the need to use wider performance measures in FM, without restricting oneself primarily to financial indicators, one could argue that each of the questions raised by Tranfield and Akhlaghi (1995) implies the need for benchmarking within FM, which, as the literature in this chapter and Chapter 9 will prove, is not easily accessible within the industry, specifically when considering the application of generic service-specific benchmarks. Tranfield and Akhlaghi (1995) consequently developed a model for benchmarking within FM, illustrating the point that benchmarking is effective when measuring both outputs and processes, and similar and dissimilar organisations.

Benchmarking in FM

A Lack of Understanding?

Although the study is a little outdated now, Massheder and Finch (1998a,b) conducted arguably the most relevant and pertinent study on the level of benchmarking in FM, concluding that it is not understood and is consequently misused by facility managers. Massheder and Finch (1998a) sent the survey to 100 companies from the top 110 operating in the United Kingdom based on capital employed (10 companies were ruled out for various reasons). The response rate was 25 percent, with 25 responses used therefore for analysis. One would argue that the response rate is fairly good; however, the actual number of responses is fairly low, and may be due to the fact that only 100 companies were targeted. As the survey is aimed at determining levels of benchmarking awareness and application within FM, Massheder and Finch added that the consequent failure of the remaining 75 percent of organisations to respond to the survey may be due to the fact that nonrespondents did not actually benchmark their FM function.

For the benefit of this study, it is worth providing a brief overview of the key findings from Massheder and Finch's research, in which the key aims of their study will be outlined below:

- *Extent to which benchmarking is used in practice*: Interestingly, only 56 percent of organisations benchmark processes associated with FM. Of those who benchmark, the most popular form of benchmarking was external strategic benchmarking.
- *Perception and use of benchmarking*: This was analysed by asking for specific words to describe their perception. The most popular words were "performance" (80%), "best practice" (76%), "cost" (76%), "quality" (76%) and "organisational improvement" (68%). Encouragingly, these are all critical words that are cross-referenced throughout this study.
- *Use of metrics*: This is analysed by asking what metrics were used across five different categories, which were business, building performance, portfolio, acquisition and disposal metrics. Massheder and Finch (1998b) are critical of the metrics used within these categories; they do not show the true efficiency that should be implemented into performance measurement systems, reiterating Massheder and Finch's point about measuring only indicators that are important to the core business.

- *The results of benchmarking in FM*: Massheder and Finch (1998b) found that benchmarking within FM is still clearly in its infancy, and a more holistic approach is needed where information is drawn from other parts of the organisation.

From Massheder and Finch's study, it is clear that improvements are needed to ensure that FM benchmarking is supported by more holistic performance measurement systems. Enoma and Allen (2007) support this view by stating that "all measurement must relate physical, functional and financial attributes on the one hand and also consider customer satisfaction, flexibility and productivity on the other" (p. 298).

From Measurement to Management

According to Enoma and Allen (2007), the concept of performance measurement has been embraced in FM, and it is increasingly used to benchmark the effectiveness of its measurement. This is true; however, to what extent has it been embraced, and how is it developing? To reinforce this, Tucker and Smith (2008) contend that

performance is moving away from the simple ideology of using metrics and costs, or any type of measurement as a 'measurement' in isolation. This is evolving into the conceptual nature of FM thinking, with the general ideology that if performance measurement is to be effective, and complementary to strategic FM, then we must make a transition from performance measurement into performance management.

One of the first leading thinkers within FM around this concept was Varcoe (1996), who emphasised that the performance measures put in place by FM organisations should be proactive and reactive to change. In other words, they should be dynamic, and measures should be constantly adjusted to focus on the critical areas that are important to the organisation. This should take into account measures that are important today and in the near future. To reinforce this point, Varcoe emphasises that organisations should measure only things that are important to measure: in other words, measures that directly assist in improving an organisation's strategic goals. To conclude this point, one would argue that if key performance measures are just "nice to know," then they should be omitted and re-evaluated. This, in essence, provides the foundation to achieving a dynamic and strategic performance measurement system. One could argue that this notion by Varcoe

(1996) has been developed further by Amaratunga *et al.* (2000), who highlight the "continually changing facilities environment" (p. 68) that has been influenced by the way the contemporary workplace is changing through the greater influence of employee behaviour and expectations, new work processes and changes in technology. Amaratunga *et al.* (2000) urge FM organisations to respond to these demands by implementing effective performance management systems to do the following:

- Translate the FM vision into clear measurable outcomes that define success and that are shared throughout the FM organisation and with its customers.
- Provide a tool for assessing, managing and improving the overall health and success of FM systems.
- Continue to shift from perspective-, audit- and compliance-based oversight to ongoing, forward-looking strategic partnerships.
- Include measures of quality, cost, speed, customer service and employee alignment, motivation and skills to provide an in-depth, predictive performance management system.
- Replace existing assessment models with a consistent approach to performance (p. 69).

Amaratunga and Baldry (2002a) suggest that the essence of performance management can be explained by the fact that "measurement is not an end to itself, but a tool for more effective management" (p. 218). The point they are making is that performance measurement must have an end meaning; it must be able to provide an explanation, and a subsequent action to its delivery. Hence, Amaratunga and Baldry (2002a) contend that to make the effective transition from measurement to management, two performance elements must be in place: the right organisational structure, which facilitates the use of performance measurement, and the ability to use performance measurement results to bring about change in the organisation.

What Performance Indicators?

Benchmarking performance within FM first became apparent in 1984, when the IFMA began collecting data and established KPIs across different FM sectors (Loosemore and Hsin, 2001). This later expanded with other organisations, such as the BIFM publishing data on FM performance. The BIFM now currently operates the "BIFM and ARK Key Performance Indicator (KPI) Register for Facilities Management", which is essentially a list of services at various levels, ranging from the top-level heading of the FM service to the range of activities within that service line and a range of indicators to measure the activities.

But the contention here is "How applicable are these measures to FM organisations, and how many companies adhere to them?" There are difficulties in obtaining a bespoke set of measurements within FM. Most notably, this argument has come from Hinks and McNay (1999), who sought to identify a bespoke set of KPIs for a financial services company; the study aimed to "overcome the known difficulties with performance measurement caused by the lack of generalised sets of data or industry wide sets of KPIs" (p. 32). The company did attempt to compare performance across other organisations; however, it found it difficult to do this effectively. The complexity of this debate can be further discouraged by contending that although there is a strive to obtain generic KPIs within FM, because of the difficulty in variance between FM organisations and sectors, sometimes this is just not possible, and we need to accept that each organisation and sector will need to be 'measured' in slightly different ways.

New Challenges and Opportunities

Invest in the Social Age and Learn More from Your Customers

We now live in the social age, where news is tailored to our preference. We no longer search for news; the news finds us (Qualman, 2009). This cataclysmic trend is the result of the increasing use of social networks, such as Facebook, Twitter and LinkedIn, in order to transfer and exchange information. The use of such platforms is becoming increasingly popular within FM, and it can be argued that 'investing time in social media actually makes you more productive' (Qualman, 2009). This is because the quality of the information that companies and customers are receiving is often quicker and more profound (Qualman, 2009). To this, it is urged that companies evaluate the ways in which they send and receive information, especially regarding performance data.

Closely linked to this shift to the social age is FM organisations' ability to learn more from their customers through better customer performance measurement. FM is centred on people – those delivering and receiving FM services. Measuring customer satisfaction is, therefore, vital to improve service delivery. However, what is astonishing within FM is that more attention is not given to the measurement of customer satisfaction with FM service delivery.

The services sector now dominates economies in the developed world. The UK services sector accounts for around 70% of gross domestic product, with private sector services alone accounting for over 50% of gross domestic product (Office for National Statistics, 2000). Within this vast market, it is clear that customers' interest in the makeup of services has changed, and now more than ever it is important for FM companies to react to this change.

Parasuraman (2004) contends that service quality fails when there is a gap between customers' service expectations and their perceptions, which are typically related to expectations of service standards, performance, and communications to customers. Hence, if customer focus is not prioritised by business, customer expectations will result in a negative disconfirmation from their perceptions, and customers will inevitably move to the next best competitor. Reflecting on the concept of the balanced scorecard (Kaplan and Norton, 1996), one could therefore contend that, particularly within the service sector, customer satisfaction remains a paramount performance measure for service delivery, and should be considered in harmony with financial, business processes and learning and growth indicators.

Case Study: Aligning Customer Satisfaction to Business Strategy

Tucker and Pitt (2009b) contend that the level of performance measurement research in FM that focuses on customer satisfaction is fairly limited. This is becoming increasingly more alarming as customer networking has become such a dominant force in company growth because companies are still grappling with the new revolutionary transformation of social age competition. Moreover, it could be argued that methods of gaining customer satisfaction within FM tend to be quantitative in nature (Sarshar and Pitt, 2009), focusing on customer satisfaction surveys, and can miss out on important issues. The initial research undertaken by Tucker and Pitt (2009a,b, 2010) in the United Kingdom and Ireland attempted to overcome these background issues through the development of a customer performance measurement system (CPMS), which incorporates both quantitative and qualitative methods of collecting customer satisfaction.

Tucker and Pitt (2009a,b, 2010) explain that the CPMS model consists of four stages. Stage 1 determines an external customer opinion through the generic benchmarks within the FM industry. Stage 2 is an internal benchmarking exercise within an individual FM organisation; this requires access to their customers and largely mimics the content of Stage 1 so comparisons can be made. A qualitative assessment is also undertaken of key FM staff within the organisation, and a sample of their customers, to further understand the current organisational framework for capturing customer satisfaction. Stage 3 analyses the data from Stages 2 and 3 and makes recommendations for change; finally, Stage 4 allows strategic decisions to be made by the organisation to devise new processes that will enhance their service provision.

For the case study, data were collected from two national quantitative surveys to obtain information on individual FM services using ordinal questions to rank each FM service by the following variables:

- *Efficiency*: the extent to which standards exceeded, or didn't exceed, expectations
- *Criticality*: the extent to which services were important to overall business operations in the occurrence of temporary failure to deliver
- *Service provision*: whether services were provided in-house or outsourced

- *Innovation*: the extent to which the level of innovation in service provision exceeded, or didn't exceed, expectations
- *Aspects of FM team*: the extent to which standards of people involvement and cultural fit, training and guidance, and general attitude exceeded, or didn't exceed, expectations.

Tucker and Pitt (2009b) found, through a series of statistical tests analysing the relationships between these variables, that only a small proportion of services actually produced significant relationships between the level of *criticality*, *efficiency* and *provision* of services. However, more significant relationships were found between the *efficiency* of services and the *aspects of the FM team* delivering the services. This suggests that customers are conscious about the people delivering the services onsite, implying that it is important for FM organisations to choose the right staff in order to achieve higher levels of customer satisfaction. Equally, there were many significant relationships evident regarding the *efficiency* of services and the level of *innovation* in service provision, suggesting that customers are conscious of how innovative FM providers are in delivering certain services. Engaging employees to understand these findings may address this relationship by more effectively guiding their innovation.

In addition to the quantitative benchmarks, Tucker and Pitt (2010) undertook 11 face-to-face qualitative interviews with the case study organisation, consisting of senior staff (4), operational staff (4) and clients (3), to gain their understanding and opinion of the benchmarking data. Generally, the key themes listed in Table 8.1 were frequently discussed through the interviews.

A briefing report was then produced, suggesting recommendations that the case study could make to help enhance their existing customer performance measurement processes, based on the quantitative benchmarks and interview data. A summary of the recommendations is as follows:

- Benchmark customer satisfaction of service delivery across individual service variables on a permanent basis.
- Incorporate a wider dissemination of benchmarking information across the company.
- Review existing customer satisfaction survey content.
- Review existing monthly customer satisfaction survey processes.
- Consider innovative strategies to demonstrate a proactive approach to improving service delivery.
- Build on existing positive relationships with clients; for example, implement further awareness sessions for staff and clients.
- Consider nominating a performance champion to amalgamate and analyse local site data and disseminate it across the company (Tucker and Pitt, 2010).

Table 8.1   Key themes

Main theme	Subthemes
The importance of customer satisfaction	*Staff–client relationships*: these were positively mentioned with regard to the focus on relationship building with clients and how the organisation has developed open and informal relationships. *Client expectations*: clients suggested that the organisation could take a more proactive approach to problems and understand the wider client view, not just that of the main contact.
Effectiveness of current processes	*Frequency of surveys*: clients get 'survey fatigue' from monthly surveys, although they do have positive face-to-face monthly meetings that clients value. *Content of surveys*: questions were too abstract or broad, and needed to drill down further to specific services and departments. *Different systems*: some clients complete one survey per contract, whilst others complete one survey per site, which skews the wider client view.
Feeding back on customer satisfaction	*Disseminating information*: clients receive local site data through positive monthly action-planning meetings but no company-wide data due to a lack of staff resources to undertake such analysis. *Linking information to strategy*: some comments discussed the uncertainty of what happens to customer satisfaction data once captured.
Benchmarking customer satisfaction	*Potential benefits*: having comparable industry standards; help with innovation and improvement; could stimulate competition when tendering for contracts

The effectiveness and applicability of the proposed CPMS model were then assessed by the case study organisation by undertaking a qualitative interviewing exercise via interviews with strategic staff only. The key outcomes are shown in Table 8.2.

In summary,

this case study shows that investing in a strategic framework to measure customer satisfaction should not be neglected or taken for granted within FM companies' performance measurement strategy. This has never been so paramount than in today's social business environment.

Table 8.2 Company outcomes

Main theme	Subthemes
Usefulness of a customer performance measurement system (CPMS)	*CPMS process*: CPMS was robust in capturing quantitative and qualitative feedback, and it was simple to understand. *Recommendations*: these were manageable and constructive, and would influence new processes. *Benchmarking surveys*: these could help compare against industry standards and stimulate innovation. Could be improved through more detail on service areas. *Qualitative interviews*: these made the process more personal by understanding perceptions beyond a standard survey approach.
Influencing changes to existing processes	*Performance measurement processes*: revision of frequency and content of surveys, and looking at new ways of disseminating analysis and output. *Company culture*: CPMS changed the perception of the organisation by embedding a customer-focused culture through a more strategic focus and by taking action to invigorate staff. *Communication*: improvements to be made on feedback through wider dissemination of information. *Service delivery*: CPMS findings indirectly impacted the company decision to relocate the 'helpdesk' service within the business. *Strategic decisions*: recruitment of Performance Director; formalising the importance of customer satisfaction
Implementation of the CPMS model	*Positive comments*: CPMS impacted the company's overall strategy through the recruitment of a Performance Director and urged them to think about adopting some key changes to their existing process.

Summary and Conclusions

Performance measurement is concerned with the process of collecting and analysing related data that will help measure predetermined goals, in order to understand the level or extent to which these goals have been achieved and, further, how these goals can be further improved. Benchmarking has become a crucial tool in measuring the performance of businesses as it allows them to gain an external understanding of how they compare to related competitors. Benchmarking can also have an overall impact on the customer satisfaction of an organisation as the organisation can aspire to gain superiority over its competitors by consistently improving standards. The nature of how we measure performance has changed over time, as it is no longer viable to rely solely on financial (quantitative) indicators, but it is necessary to gain a more strategic balance of performance measures through nonfinancial (qualitative) indicators.

The rapid growth of the services industry has had a major impact on stimulating the changing nature of performance measurement indicators, as the intangibility of services has meant that a range of indicators are necessary that not only focus on cost and value but also focus on processes and people. The introduction of the balanced scorecard has had a major influence in determining this change. The key is to measure performance based on a balanced set of indicators – financial, customer, business processes and learning and growth. This allows organisations to become more visionary and strategic in their service delivery.

Traditional performance measures tend to be narrowly focused on financial outputs, with reluctance to look at a balanced scorecard approach. This has tended to be case within the FM industry.

FM performance measurement needs to go beyond the narrow focus of the physical infrastructure and numerical measures that focus on the organisation, not the building. Understanding the importance of measuring people, processes and place within an organisation and their integration to the core business function will improve the efficiency of measuring the quality of FM services. Incorporating benchmarking into FM service delivery can create added value to overall performance measurement systems. However, it can be contested that benchmarking in FM is not understood and is consequently misused by facility managers. Being able to understand that benchmarking can be applied to wider areas of performance measurement, and not restricting it to cost-orientated measures, can significantly improve the FM function.

Performance management is an important concept to consider in FM and is strongly linked to understanding the processes involved in measuring services. When measuring FM services, we need to consider not only what the data are saying but also why they are saying it, and what we can do about it. This should be strongly linked to the organisation's core objectives.

Generic benchmarking data within FM are not widely apparent and are largely discouraged by that fact that although there is a need to obtain bespoke KPIs within FM, this is very difficult to achieve considering the variance between FM organisations and sectors, in which each organisation and sector will need to be 'measured' in slightly different ways.

There is a need to move away from traditional numerical measures to wider process measures that focus on improving the quality of service delivery, with an emphasis on people, processes and place. Customer satisfaction has emerged as a critical performance measurement component in an era that is dominated by the service sector and, more prominently, social age competition. The level of satisfaction attributed to customers is based on the difference between their initial expectations of a service and their consequent perceptions once the service is delivered.

References

Amaratunga, D., and Baldry, D. (2000). Assessment of facilities management performance in higher education properties. *Facilities*. 18(7/8), 293–301.

Amaratunga, D., and Baldry, D. (2002a). Moving from performance measurement to performance management. *Facilities*. 20(5/6), 217–223.

Amaratunga, D., and Baldry, D. (2002b). Performance measurement in facilities management and its relationships with management theory and motivation. *Facilities*. 20(10), 327–336.

Amaratunga, D., Baldry, D., and Sarshar, M. (2000). Assessment of facilities management performance – what next? *Facilities*. 18(1/2), 66–75.

Amaratunga, D., Baldry, D., and Sarshar, M. (2001). Process improvement through performance measurement: the balanced scorecard methodology. *Work Study*. 50(5), 178–188.

Camp, R.C. (1989). *Benchmarking: the search for industry best practices that lead to superior performance*. New York: ASQC Quality Press.

de Waal, A.A. (2003). The future of the balanced scorecard: an interview with Professor Dr Robert S. Kaplan. *Measuring Business Excellence*. 7(1), 30–35.

Enoma, A., and Allen, S. (2007). Developing key performance indicators for airport safety and security. *Facilities*. 25(7), 296–315.

Fitzgerald, L., and Moon, P. (1991). *Performance measurement in service businesses*. Surrey: CIMA, Black Bear Press Ltd.

Hinks, J., and McNay, P. (1999). The creation of a management-by-variance tool for facilities management performance assessment. *Facilities*. 17(1/2), 31–53.

Jones, K., and Sharp, M. (2007). A new performance-based process model for built asset maintenance. *Facilities*. 25(13/14), 525–535.

Kaplan, R.S., and Norton, D.P. (1996). *The balanced scorecard: translating strategy into action*. Boston, MA: Harvard Business School Press.

Loosemore, M., and Hsin, Y.Y. (2001). Customer-focused benchmarking for facilities management. *Facilities*. 19(13/14), 464–475.

Massheder, K., and Finch, E. (1998a). Benchmarking methodologies applied to UK facilities management. *Facilities*. 16(3/4), 99–106.

Massheder, K., and Finch, E. (1998b). Benchmarking metrics used in UK facilities management. *Facilities*. 16(5/6), 123–127.

McDougall, G., and Hinks, J. (2000). Identifying priority issues in facilities management benchmarking. *Facilities*. 18(10/11/12), 427–434.

Neely, A. (1999). The performance measurement revolution: why now and what next? *International Journal of Operations and Production Management*. 19(2), 205–228.

Office for National Statistics. (2000). *The UK Service Sector*. London: Office for National Statistics.

Parasuraman, A. (2004). Assessing and improving service performance for maximum impact: insights from a two-decade-long research journey. *Performance Measurement and Metrics*. 5(2), 45–52.

Price, I., and Akhlaghi, F. (1999). New patterns in facilities management: industry best practice and new organisational theory. *Facilities*. 17(5/6), 159–166.

Sarshar, M., and Pitt, M. (2009). Adding value to clients: learning from four case studies. *Facilities*. 27(9/10), 399–412.

Tranfield, D., and Akhlaghi, F. (1995). Performance measures: relating facilities to business indicators. *Facilities.* 13(3), 6–14.

Tucker, M., and Pitt, M. (2009a). Customer performance measurement in facilities management: a strategic approach. *International Journal of Productivity and Performance Management.* 56(5), 407–442.

Tucker, M., and Pitt, M. (2009b). National standards of customer satisfaction in facilities management. *Facilities.* 27(13/14), 497–415.

Tucker, M., and Pitt, M. (2010). Improving service provision through better management and measurement of customer satisfaction in facilities management. *Journal of Corporate Real Estate.* 12(4), 220–233.

Tucker, M., and Smith, A. (2008). User perceptions in workplace productivity and strategic FM delivery. *Facilities.* 26(5/6), 196–212.

Varcoe, B.J. (1996). Facilities performance measurement. *Facilities.* 14(10/11), 46–51.

Zairi, M. (1994). Benchmarking: the best tool for measuring competitiveness. *Benchmarking for Quality Management and Technology.* 1(1), 11–24.

Industry-Specific Needs

Sarel Lavy and Manish Dixit

Texas A&M University, College Station, TX

This chapter covers facility management (FM) in four major industries: education facilities, public sector buildings, healthcare facilities, and office buildings. Even though common themes may be found among these four major types of facilities, there are still some significant differences among them that are addressed throughout the course of this chapter. This chapter is structured as a literature review that provides the current state of the art of FM research.

Education Facilities

An Education Facility's Condition and Students' Performance

The performance of students as well as teachers is affected by the quality of their physical environment. Research has found a strong positive correlation between the condition of a school facility and the achievement of its students. Studies suggest that there is a significant difference (5–17 percentile points) between the achievement levels of students studying in poor and standard school conditions, if socioeconomic factors are controlled (Earthman, 2002; Young *et al.*, 2003; American Federation of Teachers, 2006; Cash and Twiford, 2009; Collins and Parson, 2010). The adverse impact on physical health results in absenteeism and poor academic performance, and it affects teachers, resulting in poor productivity and a low retention rate. Some prominent negative impacts on students' and teachers' physical health

International Facility Management, First Edition. Kathy O. Roper and Lisa J. Borello.
© 2014 John Wiley & Sons, Ltd. Published 2014 by John Wiley & Sons, Ltd.

might include asthma, cold, fatigue, nausea, vomiting, drowsiness, aggravated allergies, a range of respiratory infections, increased stress levels, negative attitude, lack of discipline, lack of attention, and violent behavior.

A variety of factors can affect the condition of a school facility. Young *et al.* (2003) categorized it into three categories: physical, spatial, and environmental. Physical factors relate to the physical condition of a school, which includes interior and exterior conditions, such as the age of the building and its components, structural damage, leakage, cracks, expired building components, and so on. Spatial factors relate to the adequacy of a space to fulfill a particular function, and lack of proper space management. The issues relating to the condition of a space such as general cleanliness, indoor air quality, lighting, thermal comfort, and noise are considered to be environmental factors. Any single physical, spatial, or environmental factor might cause a range of adverse impacts on a student's health, affecting his or her academic performance.

The issues with school facilities that are raised by the literature can be addressed by applying strategies such as flexible design, enforcing rigorous maintenance and replacement policies, and installing modern equipment (Lyons, 2001). Lack of funds in poor economic times could be a major hindrance in applying these strategies. Cash and Twiford (2009) suggested various strategies to improve the condition of a school facility in a cost-effective manner. Most of these strategies include effective maintenance and replacement activities by a well-trained custodian and maintenance staff personnel (Schneider, 2002).

Energy Management in Schools and Other Educational Facilities

Education facilities in the United States consumed nearly 10.5% of the total energy used by all building sectors in 2003 (US Department of Energy (USDOE), 2010c). K–12 school facilities in the United States spend nearly $8 billion on energy use each year, which represents the second highest operating expenditure by a school facility (USDOE, 2010b; Cross *et al.*, 2011). In the 2005–2006 school year, school facilities spent nearly $1.15 per square foot, 63% and 34% of which were attributed to electricity and natural gas use, respectively (Kats, 2006; Cross *et al.*, 2011).

Reducing energy use in school facilities can bring two major benefits to society: first, it helps the nation in reducing the carbon dioxide emissions that result primarily from fossil fuel combustion; and, second, school facilities can save significant amounts of money, which may be reallocated to core purposes, such as recruiting better teachers and enhancing the learning experience of students.

In the current time of budget cuts, any potential monetary savings could help schools to spend more funds on improving the condition of their facilities and to focus on their main purpose, which is to provide quality education (Cash and Twiford, 2009; USDOE, 2010a). According to the USDOE (2010a), an independent school district with 4000 students in the United States could save up to $160,000 each year by effectively managing its energy use.

According to Cash and Twiford (2009), a typical school in the United States expends nearly 41%, 14%, and 30% of its total annual energy on space cooling, space heating, and lighting, respectively. These three components account for nearly 85% of the total energy usage, indicating the major areas of potential energy savings. A survey conducted by the American Association of School Administrators (AASA) concluded that 59% and 37% of respondents believed in implementing energy-saving measures and reducing energy use for heating and cooling, respectively, among major cost-cutting strategies (USDOE, 2010a). Operations and maintenance (O&M) practices and occupant behavior are two major components that can also bring significant energy savings to school facilities (Erickson, 2010; Cross *et al.*, 2011).

A series of documents have been published by the US Environmental Protection Agency and Department of Energy to provide step-by-step guidance on developing and implementing energy conservation programs in K–12 school facilities. The publications, such as US Environmental Protection Agency (EPA, 2011) and USDOE (2010a,b), provide detailed instruction on O&M practices that could generate significant energy savings in school facilities.

Space Usage and Planning in School Facilities

One of the major factors found to impact the performance of students and teachers in a school setting is spatial requirements (Jones, 1960; American Federation of Teachers, 2006, Earthman, 2002; McGowen, 2007). The adequacy, organization, and quality of a learning space are being affected by increasing enrollments in existing schools, resulting in overcrowding. According to the American Federation of Teachers (2006), the US Department of Education (National Center for Education Statistics) reported that nearly 8.5% of US schools have already exceeded their student capacity. As a result of overcrowding, school administration is forced to either use common areas or temporary facilities for instruction or combine the existing instructional areas to accommodate more students. Problems such as increased insubordination, less individualized attention, and lack of concentration could stem out of overcrowding of instructional spaces (American Federation of Teachers, 2006; McGowen, 2007). Douglas (1996) concluded that space is vital in deciding the functional worth of a facility, and in order for one to evaluate its suitability, a facility manager must assess its three primary aspects: amount (area and volume), quality, and shape. The assessment of space utilization is vital to identify underutilized and overutilized spaces (Douglas, 1993–1994; Schroeder et al., 1995).

The question that arises is how much space is needed or is sufficient for a school in order for it to be spatially adequate. Abramson (2006) argues that the school program, not the space goals, should govern the space requirements of a school. There could be three types of spaces in a school setting: instructional (e.g. classrooms), supplemental (e.g. laboratories), and support spaces (e.g. the gymnasium and auditorium). Each of these spaces has different space standards. The National Clearinghouse for Educational Facilities provides a series of publications on its website on space standards for school settings at various levels such as elementary, middle, and high school. The space standards are expressed in gross square foot area per student for different annual enrollments. Publications such as RIDE (2007) and Fife (2006) provide space standards for various instructional, supplemental, and support school spaces.

Safety, Security, and Disaster Recovery

The safety and security levels of a school setting can have profound impact on learning outcomes (Young et al., 2003; Cash and Twiford, 2009). Students feel more secure, safe, and confident if they observe safety and security provisions. There are various factors that could affect the safety and security level of a school. In the time of budget cuts, for instance, layoffs of security staff are quite common in many school districts (Eisele-Dyrli, 2010). In addition, to save electricity costs, significant reductions in exterior lighting, for example, made school premises unsafe and highly prone to vandalism, violence, and terror attacks (Eisele-Dyrli, 2010). The increased number of shooting events and violent and behavioral incidents in schools should be taken as serious warnings to parents, educators, and policy makers (Trump, 2004). According to Trump (2004, 2009), the increased pressure on schools to significantly improve the test scores has put safety and security issues on the back burner.

School security and safety form one of the key areas of the FM profession (NewSchools Venture Fund, 2008). Most security and disaster recovery is related to manmade incidences of violence, vandalism, hostage situation, terrorism, and fire. Major natural disasters include earthquakes and severe weather conditions, such as lightning, storms, hurricanes, tornadoes, and floods (Trump, 2004; Watson et al., 2008). Safety in a school environment mostly relates to physical and psychological harm to students, staff, and visitors, covering events such as poisoning, exposure to hazardous materials, trauma, falls, and so on (American Federation of Teachers, 2006; Trump, 2009).

One of the key strategies to deal with any unforeseen disaster situations is disaster preparedness. Informing and educating the occupants about a probable man-made or natural disaster would help in reducing fear and panic (Trump, 2004, 2009). Planning and implementation of a meaningful preparedness plan by including police, fire, emergency medical, and emergency management agencies are the most important parts of disaster preparedness. To deal with an adverse weather condition, a public alert radio (also known as a hazard alert or weather radio) is the fastest, most accurate, and most highly reliable disaster preparedness system (Watson *et al.*, 2008).

Public Sector Buildings

Use of Technology in the FM Industry

FM departments perform the job of managing the built environment, which involves up to 8–12% of an organization's total annual capital budget (Ness and Teicholz, 2000). Although the field of FM was not fully supported by technology until recently, various computer-based tools have now become available to help in routine FM tasks. Automating FM-related tasks may result in better service, higher quality, financial gains, and enhanced safety; however, automation in FM would require a change in an organization's culture and processes (Keller, 2005).

Among the major tools available today for FM to use are as follows:

CAFM: computer-aided facility management
CMMS: computerized maintenance management system
CIFM: computer-integrated facility management
CPMS: capital planning and management solutions

CAFM is a web-based tool utilizing information technology to collect and supply life-cycle information that supports decision making related to modeling, evaluation, control, and feedback on key issues (Madritsch and May, 2008). It is used for functions ranging from need analysis, through acquisition and construction, to operation, maintenance, and demolition of a built facility (JCC, 2011). A tool that focuses on the process of maintaining a facility is CMMS, which records, manages, and communicates routine maintenance procedures in a facility (Sapp, 2011). A CMMS can also help in managing the resources of an organization and in assessing the effectiveness of a facility's maintenance plan. CIFM is an integrated system that consists of a set of modules addressing various areas of FM (Bodini *et al.*, 2004). A modification made to any of these modules is automatically reflected in other relevant modules. The modules manage the information related to space, employees, user movements, the help desk, and maintenance. According to Ness and

Teicholz (2000), to estimate, track, and allocate values such as a Facility Condition Index (FCI), a CPMS could be very helpful. In addition, it can help provide required data for budget requests and for creating capital projects.

Technologies, such as geographical information system (GIS) and building information modeling (BIM), are also being used for FM-related functions. GIS, which was initially used for analyzing the impact of built facilities on the natural environment, is now being used to plan, manage, operate, and dispose of a facility (Rich and Davis, 2010). Use of a BIM has increased not only in the design and construction of a building but also in its management and operations phases (AutoDesk, 2008; General Services Administration (GSA), 2011). AutoDesk has also proposed an AutoDesk FMDesktop that can be used for FM processes to manage and track facility drawings, data, assets, occupants, and maintenance requests (AutoDesk, 2008; GSA, 2011). The US General Services Administration has proposed a guide on the use of BIM for FM (GSA, 2011). According to the guide, "BIM is a data rich, object-based, intelligent and parametric digital representation of the facility."

> Governments with large portfolios of space are leading the implementation of BIM for life-cycle management, and their guidelines are easily accessible via the Internet.

Financing of FM by Public Finance Initiatives in the Public Sector

A private finance initiative (PFI) is designed to involve the private sector in the life cycle of a public building to enhance its efficiency, effectiveness, and quality (Nutt, 2000; Allen, 2001; Baldwin, 2003; Akintoye et al., 2005). It was originally conceptualized in the United Kingdom in 1992 (Baldwin, 2003), where PFI contracts included public sector projects, such as healthcare, education, prison, defense, roads, and highways (Bennett and Iossa, 2006). In its simplest and most common form, a PFI allows the private sector to design, build, finance, and operate a public facility. Such an arrangement requires bundling the design, construction, and FM functions together to cover the entire life cycle of a facility (Bennett and Iossa, 2006; Brochner, 2008).

According to Akintoye et al. (2005), PFI is an effort to bring the public and private sectors to "share the risks and rewards." PFI also helps in transferring the risk partially or completely to the private sector. According to Nutt (2000), the primary purpose of PFI is to identify, allocate, and manage the financial risks of a facility. Another main purpose of PFI is to deliver high-quality public services through "modern and purpose-designed facilities" (Baldwin, 2003).

The share of PFI in public building expenditures is growing, as 11% of the total government expenditure in the United Kingdom in 2002 was in the form of PFI (Akintoye *et al.*, 2005). According to Bennett and Iossa (2006), the PFI investment in the United Kingdom from 1998 until 2004 ranged between 10 and 13.5% of the total investment in the public service sector. Baldwin (2003) argues that apart from providing a quality public facility and services, PFI must also ensure a return to the taxpayers and investors in the form of a value for money and profitability, respectively. Akintoye *et al.* (2005) provide a list of critical success factors (CSFs) to measure a PFI contract's success. The list of CSFs includes factors relating to risk, the procurement process, cost–benefit analysis, governance, project feasibility, economic policy, and social and political support.

Building Performance Measurement and Simulations

The measurement of a facility's performance is vital for not only assessing the current condition but also identifying measures that could enhance its future performance (Cable and Davis, 2004; Lavy *et al.*, 2010). A facility can be evaluated in terms of its functional, financial, physical, and environmental performance. Functional performance deals with the appropriateness of a facility for the desired function, whereas physical performance is linked with the overall physical condition of a facility. The operational expenditure is related to both the financial and environmental performance, as it can affect the annual operational cost, energy consumption, and health and comfort levels in the facility. Zimring (2010) asserted that facility performance assessment is known by various terms such as *postoccupancy evaluation* (POE), *building evaluation, environmental design evaluation, building performance evaluation*, and *environmental audits*. Meng and Minogue (2011) provided a comparative description of tools for measuring organizational performance, including the balanced scorecard (BSC), business excellence model (BEM), key performance indicators (KPI), and the capability maturity model (CMM).

Various computer and web-based tools are available to evaluate a building's performance over its life cycle. Tools such as BLAST, ECOTECT, TRNSYS, HOT 2000, Energy Plus, DOE 2.1 (USDOE), RIUSKA, MOIST 3.0, CONDENSE, Airpak, and hyglRC are all available to perform computer simulations to assess a built facility economically and environmentally (Crawley *et al.*, 2005; Hammad *et al.*, 2005). Most of the tools are actually Building Energy Performance Simulation (BEPS) tools focused on energy consumption (Maile *et al.*, 2010). According to Zimring (2010), the GSA collaborated with the

Center for the Built Environment (CBE) to develop a web-based tool to administer a POE survey. Current simulation tools require complex input collection that is either time-consuming or expensive, and they need advanced computer skills, professional experience, and engineering knowledge, which may not be always available (Bazjanac, 2001; Hammad *et al.*, 2005; Hamza and Horne, 2007). Hence, their use by architectural and engineering firms has been limited.

One alternative to make computer simulations user-friendly and less time consuming, especially for building design, construction, and management professionals, is to integrate them into computer-aided design tools (Hamza and Horne, 2007). Tools such as BIM are now being fused with add-in tools that could perform various building performance evaluation functions. Industry Foundation Classes (IFC) facilitate interoperability among IFC-compliant software (in the architecture, engineering, and construction industries) in order to either extract building geometry or exchange information that assists in performing building simulations (Bazjanac and Crawley, 1997; Mitchell *et al.*, 2007).

Efficient Preservation of Aged and Deteriorating Structures

Existing buildings constitute nearly 98–99% of the total building stock in most developed and developing countries like the United States, India, and China (CBRE, 2011; Paumgartten, n.d.). In Europe, new construction accounts for only 1% of the total building stock (Baek and Park, 2012). A significant portion of the existing buildings are historical buildings with associated social and cultural values (Forster and Kayan, 2009; Wang *et al.*, 2008). Preservation of such buildings requires maintenance and retrofitting activities that should be sensitive toward these values.

Baek and Park (2012) argue that the focus of renovating an old building keeps changing from social problems to environmental issues. In the past, the deteriorating physical condition of an old building was a major issue due to health and safety concerns. With time (since 1980), the focus of building renovations shifted to making old buildings suitable for elderly and disabled people. In recent times, energy consumption and waste generation issues are the focus for maintaining and renovating existing old buildings. Successful preservation of old buildings depends on periodic maintenance that underpins their survival (Forster and Kayan, 2009). Regular maintenance also needs to aim at retaining the cultural significance of the old buildings. One key strategy, suggested by Forster and Kayan (2009), is to perform proactive (preventive) maintenance, which results in long-term cost savings. Among the major benefits of implementing preventive maintenance policies are preservation of historic materials, avoidance of disturbance to surrounding fabric, avoidance of encroachments, and retention of cultural values.

Healthcare Facilities

Life-cycle Cost Analysis and Methodologies

Life-cycle cost is the sum of the present values of all costs, such as investment, capital, operating, energy, maintenance, replacement, refurbishment, and disposal costs, that incur during the period of a facility's life cycle (Fuller, 2005, 2010; Krus, 2004). Life-cycle cost analysis (LCCA) is an approach used to assess a project economically by including all costs relating to the project (Boussabaine *et al.*, 2012). LCCA is vital for making decisions, such as those relating to investment, cost optimization, and reduction of resource use.

LCCA in the case of healthcare facilities is more complicated than in other sectors because, conventionally, these facilities are expected to provide quality care at a lower cost (Kirk, 1996). To maintain the quality of indoor atmosphere and patient care, the incurred higher construction and O&M costs need to be balanced. One major cost component in the total cost of ownership of a typical hospital is salaries and wages, which accounts for up to 50% of the life-cycle cost (Kirk, 1996). Apart from salaries and wages, the O&M costs represent the largest fraction of the life-cycle costs (Boussabaine *et al.*, 2012). In a study of four hospitals, Heider and Brockman (2010) found that life-cycle costs can be influenced considerably by type of ownership (public or private), climate (extreme or mild), hospital scale, and building use (services provided). Likewise, Boussabaine *et al.* (2012) concluded that the O&M costs are highly correlated to the number of hospital beds and the gross floor area(hospital size) of the building.

The process of LCCA requires following a standard procedure (Kirk, 1996). In the United States, the American Society for Testing and Materials (ASTM) publishes documents (e.g. E917-05, "Standard Practice for Measuring Life-Cycle Costs of Buildings and Building Systems"; ASTM, 2010) providing procedural guidance on carrying out LCCA. Krus (2004) discussed various life-cycle cost models that are being used for healthcare facilities, including the American Society for Heating Refrigerating and Air-Conditioning Engineers (ASHRAE) model and the Federal Energy Management Program (FEMP) model. The ASHRAE model utilizes data sources, such as the USDOE and RS-Means, to obtain cost data for various components. The FEMP model follows the ASTM procedure, and it is the required method for LCCA for US federal facilities. The *Facilities Pricing Guide*, published by the US Department of Defense (DoD), is also used to source the initial construction and annual sustainment cost for military healthcare facilities (Krus, 2004).

O&M Strategies to Optimize FM Performance

O&M processes are required to enable a facility to perform the functions for which it was built, and it constitutes the largest fraction of the life-cycle cost of a healthcare facility, after wages and salaries (Boussabaine *et al.*, 2012). A well-worked-out and organized O&M program can optimize a facility's operations to result in sizeable savings in the consumption of resources like energy, water, and materials (Sullivan *et al.*, 2010; Sapp, 2011). It may save up to 5–20% of the annual utility bill in commercial buildings without any significant investment (Haasl, 1999; Sullivan *et al.*, 2010). Energy efficiency through operation and maintenance can help save a considerable amount of capital expenditure, and it can also enhance the operating efficiency of heating, ventilation, and air conditioning (HVAC); lighting; and other energy-using systems.

Hospitals are among the most energy-consuming commercial facilities: they function 24/7, with energy-intensive medical equipment and a well-maintained, healthy, and comfortable indoor atmosphere (Schneider Electric, 2006; Singer and Tschudi, 2009). The processes of water heating, space conditioning, and lighting in a typical healthcare facility can account for 61–79% of the total energy use, depending on the climate type (American Society for Healthcare Engineering (ASHE), 2004). Energy consumption is a major factor in rising operating costs of a typical hospital facility (ASHE, 2004; Schneider Electric, 2006). Meanwhile, facility managers are working with ever-shrinking budgets to meet O&M requirements in spite of increasing costs of energy, water, materials, and labor (Lavy and Shohet, 2004; Saporta *et al.* 2008).

The American Society of Healthcare Engineers (ASHE, 2004) discusses two approaches to reduce energy consumption and eventually the operating expenditures of a healthcare facility. First, a management approach is required to control the need for energy supply, called "demand-side management." This can be accomplished by changing the light fixtures, HVAC system, and building equipment, and by installing advanced controls to regulate the use of HVAC and other equipment. Second is a management approach to procure and supply the needed energy in the most cost-effective and efficient manner, known as "supply-side management." Some strategies suggested to manage the supply of energy include load profiling, load aggregation, onsite energy generation (cogeneration), finding alternative cost-effective energy suppliers, and peak load reduction. Other recommended strategies include diversified power sources, deregulation, and outsourcing energy management. Singer and Tschudi (2009) list various challenges to energy-efficient O&M related to medical services, healthcare organizations (structure and culture), the legacy of current hospital facility stock, and codes and standards.

For effective and efficient maintenance management of a healthcare facility, a CMMS can be very useful (Gomez and Carnero, 2011). CMMS helps in the management of information relating to maintenance schedule, workforce, inventories, and equipment records. It can also automate maintenance procedures by planning and scheduling the work order system. A variety of software is available to select from for the purpose of CMMS. Gomez and Carnero (2011) provided a list of criteria for selecting the right software for CMMS of a hospital building. It is also important to measure the maintenance performance of a healthcare facility in order to make changes in future implementation of the maintenance program.

Maximizing Value during Predesign, Delivery, and Construction

According to Vittori (2011), healthcare expenditure in the United States, which is currently 17% of the gross domestic product (GDP), is expected to grow up to 25% of GDP by the end of 2025.

It is evident that the built environment created by hospital buildings affects the health and comfort of the hospital staff and also influences patients' healing (Stichler, 2010; Sadler *et al.*, 2011). Hence, to maximize value during the predesign, delivery, and construction phases, efforts should be focused on making a hospital facility sustainable in all aspects: economically, environmentally, and socially (Kahn, 2009).

In order to achieve this goal, those who are close to the point of service should be involved in each stage of the project delivery (Stichler, 2010). To generate a high-performing hospital design, involvement of an interdisciplinary design and construction team in the healthcare project delivery is very important. Such teams could be well integrated into any value-maximizing project delivery system, such as design-build or integrated project delivery (IPD) (Kahn, 2009). Inputs from a representative of the FM department and the nursing department are essential to increase economic, environmental, health, and comfort benefits (Stichler, 2010). Facility managers are well aware of building materials, systems, equipment, communication, and hospital utilities (e.g. energy supply, water, information, drugs, and medical gases) (Patterson, 2008). Their involvement in the predesign, design, and construction phases can help reduce a hospital's long-term maintenance and operating costs (Patterson, 2008).

The role of equipment planning during a hospital's design and construction phases is also emphasized to generate financial savings due to a reduced number of change orders, an equipment-specific budget, equipment efficiency and technology, and upfront planning of required engineering and architectural provisions (Beney, 1999). According to Ticer (2011), medical equipment planning has three major milestones, which occur at the preliminary budget planning, end of design development, and project closeout (project management signoff) stages. Sadler *et al.* (2011) discussed the "Fable hospital," an imaginary hospital design solution incorporating the best design innovations. They also concluded that such a design approach may result in fewer patient falls, fewer staff injuries, reduced nursing turnover, fewer patient transfers, reduced hospital-acquired infections, reduced resource (energy and water) use, reduced length of patient stay, and less adverse drug events. All of these impacts have the potential to generate significant financial savings, and they may provide a safe, healthy, comfortable, and more productive healthcare environment.

FM Strategies for Infection Control in Healthcare Facilities

Hospital-acquired infection has now become a prevailing worldwide problem in healthcare facilities (Evans and Henderson, 2005). According to Riley *et al.* (2006), over 2 million patients in the United States alone suffer from hospital-acquired infections, and over 88,000 of them die each year. All users of healthcare facilities, including patients, medical staff, administrative staff, and visitors, are exposed to a range of infections (Bartley, 2000; Noskin and Peterson, 2001; London Mallee Region (LMR), 2003). Other users, such as contractors and workers involved in maintenance or renovation work, are also at risk. On the other hand, construction activities relating to renovation in a fully functional healthcare facility could pose infection hazards to patients, due to dust generation and water contamination or spill (LMR, 2003). During the use phase, the FM division of a hospital deals with routine maintenance and repair work, and it is also responsible for major decisions relating to renovation works. Facility managers are also involved in facility operations relating to HVAC and water supply. Such activities greatly affect the spread of infection in a healthcare environment (Bartley, 2000; LMR, 2003; Riley *et al.*, 2006).

Unfortunately, hospital-acquired infections are associated with a significant number of deaths each year. Prevention measures, such as design strategies for infection control, environmental control guidelines, improved HVAC systems, and FM strategies for infection control in maintenance and renovation processes, can be used to reduce the spread of infection (Bartley, 2000; Noskin and Peterson, 2001; LMR, 2003). Most of the design strategies can be applied during the design phase, where healthcare facility managers' input is considered significant. The selection of wall materials and ceiling and floor finishes in a hospital environment should be done on the basis of use of the space (wear and tear), risk of harboring infection (e.g. water-absorbing, porous, or fibrous material may harbor bacteria and germs), and ease of cleaning (Bartley, 2000; Noskin and Peterson, 2001; Riley *et al.*, 2006). A FM professional who is well aware of material properties can help select the appropriate finishes, considering infection control hazards.

Regular maintenance and upkeep of the HVAC and air distribution system, with the use of high-efficiency particulate air (HEPA) filters that can capture particles of $0.3\,\mu m$ diameter, can effectively reduce the risk of infection spread (Evans and Henderson, 2005). The amount of outside air that needs to be supplied to the hospital should be determined and checked regularly. If any construction or renovation activity is going on, it needs to be isolated by creating a negative pressure in the construction zone (Bartley, 2000). Some airborne pathogenic fungi (e.g. *Aspergillus fumigatus*) are contained in dust that could damage the sterile healthcare environment (LMR, 2003). Fungi can also grow on materials such as gypsum boards on the wall or ceiling, if the surfaces are kept wet for long time (Riley *et al.*, 2006). Therefore, if water leakages occur, they should be addressed immediately.

Before starting any renovation, construction, or major repair activity in a functional hospital environment, a multidisciplinary team that includes an architect, facility manager, infection control professional (ICP), senior representative of the client department, and project manager should be formed (LMR, 2003; Riley *et al.*, 2006). Communication between clinical and engineering staff is also significant during such activities. The first major task for the team is to conduct a risk assessment that involves identifying major risks and those who are at risk; the next strategy is planning and controlling the infection control risks. Strategies such as work sequencing, physical isolation of a renovation or construction zone, planning for utility outages, addressing potential penetrations in exterior and interior walls, and noise and vibration reduction may be helpful in managing infection risks (LMR, 2003; Riley *et al.*, 2006). The facility personnel and construction workers should be educated about potential harmful infections, and they must be trained to work in an infectious environment (Bartley, 2000). Personal protective equipment is to be provided, and workers should be encouraged to use it while working on a maintenance or renovation job.

Office Buildings

Changing Office Work Patterns

The work pattern in today's office environment is changing rapidly with changing ways of communication, business, and management (Tanis and Duffy, 1999; Miller, 2001; Ware and Grantham, 2003; Palmer, 2012). Work has been changing in terms of its structure, content, and process.

It has become more mobile, cognitively complex, collaborative, social skills based, technology based, and time pressured (Heerwagen *et al.*, 2005). Today's organizations are also changing rapidly and becoming more agile, leaner, more customer focused, more strategic, and less hierarchical, and they are continually reorganizing due to changing competition (Ware and Grantham, 2003; Andrew *et al.*, 2008). A change in organization is also affecting work and the physical workplace greatly. According to Ware and Grantham (2003), organizations are trying to create a working environment that attracts highly motivated and high-performing workers, while simultaneously reducing the cost of workforce support.

The work pattern is changing in terms of time, space, and technology, with questions such as "When to work?", "Where to work?", and "How to work?" Concepts such as videoconferencing and teleworking, or working from a place other than the office, are gaining more popularity (Tanis and Duffy, 1999; Miller 2001). Working hours are becoming more flexible and provide more working alternatives to employees, which may also satisfy the demand of customers for goods and services at times other than regular business hours (Advisory, Conciliation and Arbitration Service (ACAS), 2005). Part-time work, overtime, flextime (in which employees choose their work time), weekend working, flexible working weeks, career breaks, and working while commuting are becoming common in the current work environment (ACAS, 2005). Concepts such as job sharing (more than one worker sharing the same job), shiftwork, a flexible work contract (to be used whenever needed), temporary working, subcontracting, and zero-hour working are also changing the workplace (ACAS, 2005). Technology is also changing rapidly, and it is gradually affecting the way we work today. The penetration of the web (e.g. social media), mobile applications, laptops, and other advanced and wireless office equipment can be seen as among the major factors contributing to this change in work patterns (Tanis and Duffy, 1999; ACAS, 2005; Palmer, 2012). A change is also being observed in the work team configurations that are influencing the workplace. According to Miller (2001), a linear team pattern performs jobs by passing on the finished tasks, whereas a parallel team is made of different departments with specialized skills working on different projects. Circular teams are created for innovation as they work collaboratively with team members, coming and going as needed.

Changing workplace patterns can affect employee learning, satisfaction, and productivity greatly by providing a distraction-free workspace and opportunity for learning through interactions. Andrew *et al.* (2008) reported that a study conducted by Scheider (2007) found an increase of 21% in organizational productivity with an improved workplace. Such changes in the organization, work, workplaces, and work patterns certainly affect the way that facility managers operate and maintain office environments. Duffy (2000) argued that facility managers and designers have equal responsibility for creating a workplace environment that is conducive to its employees, and compares FM and architectural design by stating that "as software is to hardware, so facilities management is to design."

Adaptability and Productivity in Office Spaces

The spatial, functional, and environmental qualities of an office space affect employee satisfaction, which eventually influences organizational productivity and also the churn (turnover) rate. Haynes (2008) cited and discussed research (Gensler, 2005) concluding that an office environment conducive to its users can increase productivity by nearly 19%. Moreover, nearly 89% of respondents associated the office environment with their job satisfaction in a study conducted by Gensler (2005). Employees require creative and productive spaces that provide them with distraction-free workspace, individual controls, a sense of ownership, privacy, the opportunity to interact and collaborate, and flexibility to meet the demands of ever-changing technology (Gensler, 2005; Haynes, 2008; O'Neill, 2008). A rapid change in organizations, innovative and contemporary workplace designs, and growing environmentally friendly concerns have all emphasized the significance of adaptability of an office space (Arge, 2005; Bullen and Love, 2011).

Three aspects of physical design of office buildings exist: (1) generality, which means that the proposed design can be used for a range of functions; (2) flexibility, which means that the building properties can be changed easily to meet the changing needs of users; and (3) elasticity, which allows the modification of space configuration by shifting or extending partitions (Arge, 2005). Brand (1998) argued that, unfortunately, emphasis is given to space performance (accommodating more users in a limited space) rather than to human performance. Bullen and Love (2011) claimed that reconfiguration is certainly better than relocation as it is less disruptive. Moreover, a less flexible building is less valuable than an adaptable building. A two-tiered approach is proposed by Brand (1998) that included a long-term (to meet changing and growing work patterns) and a short-term (to support current functions) perspective in making office facilities flexible.

How do facility managers address the changing demands of users of an office environment? Brand (1998) provided a four-way strategy for facility managers to deal with the issue of adaptability. First, it was suggested to fully utilize whatever is available as a resource (e.g. space, furniture, and equipment). This can be accomplished by reconfiguration of space by applying an ergonomics program and employing a qualified interior designer to make the reconfigured office environment functionally, environmentally, and socially conducive. Second, work areas should be designed as functioning spaces rather than individual footprints.

Designing an office space that can house individuals, as well as team-work spaces, is essential for employee learning; according to Brand (1998), nearly 60% of skills are learned by employees by informal inter-action. Third, spaces should provide individuals more control on furni-ture layout, equipment, communication, thermal comfort, and lighting. This provides a sense of ownership to employees and increases their satisfaction. Finally, configuring space to support team as well as private work was considered vital for improving productivity. This poses issues for space management but is a vital component of knowledge work in today's offices.

Ventilation in Office Buildings

It has been discussed that the physical environment of a work space affects workers' satisfaction and eventually their productivity. One major factor that can affect the productivity of a worker is indoor air quality (Wargocki et al., 2000; Seppanen et al., 2006; Tsai et al., 2012). Indoor air is continually contaminated by harmful emissions (e.g. volatile organic compounds, or VOCs) from building materials (e.g. finishes), human beings (e.g. tobacco smoking), and office equipment (e.g. photo-copiers) (Daisey et al., 1994). These contaminants make air unhealthy, causing various health effects such as lethargy, headaches, rash, irritation, and upper respiratory symptoms, among others (Jaakkola and Miettinen, 1995; Tsai et al., 2012). Most of these effects are common symptoms of sick building syndrome (SBS), which is a major problem of poor indoor air quality. Outside air ventilation can be used to dilute the amount of contaminants in the indoor air (Wargocki et al., 2000; Seppanen et al., 2006). A low ventilation rate in office buildings has been associated with increased cases of SBS and other infectious diseases (Seppanen et al., 2006). The quality of indoor air is dependent on the amount of clean outside air supplied to the office space, and it also affects workers' comfort, health, and satisfaction (Bennett et al., 2012).

Outside air can be provided in the form of mechanical or natural ventilation to dilute the concentration of indoor air contaminants (Chang et al., 2004; Gail et al., 2011). If outside air conditions are favorable, a considerable amount of cooling and heating can also be obtained by supplying the outside air. Among major challenges to the use of natural ventilation in an office atmosphere are its limited applica-bility due to numerous building and climate types. Some office building may house functions that are sensitive to increased humidity. In climates with high humidity, outside air intake might make indoor atmosphere uncomfortably humid (Gail et al., 2011). Mechanical ventilation utilizes mechanically induced drafts of air to supply outside air.

The American Society of Heating, Refrigerating and Air-Conditioning Engineers (ASHRAE) publishes and periodically updates standards for ensuring indoor air quality in commercial buildings, including office buildings. Ventilation for Acceptable Indoor Air Quality (ANSI/ASHRAE Standard 62.1-2010) is the current standard that provides guidelines for supplying the minimum required outside air based on the office area and number of occupants in the office space. Bennett *et al.* (2012) conducted a study of 37 small commercial buildings and found that nearly 38% of the buildings did not have a supply of outside air either due to the absence of an outside air intake or because the outside air damper was forced shut. Nearly 18% and 53% of the studied buildings did not comply with ASHRAE 62.1 standards at the actual and default occupancy levels, respectively. Their study also found that particle filters used in the HVAC system were of low efficiency. According to the EPA (1991), pollen, dust, fungal spores, industrial pollutants, and vehicle exhaust are among major sources of exterior pollutants that can enter the indoor atmosphere if proper filters are not used.

FM professionals provide the direct link between building operations and maintenance activities and the quality and amount of outside air supplied to the office spaces. They are also responsible for the overall quality of the indoor atmosphere by ensuring pollutant-free and low-contaminant indoor air. The operations and maintenance of HVAC and air distribution systems greatly affect the indoor air quality (EPA, 1991). Moreover, periodic replacement of filters is vital for ensuring clean supply of air to the office spaces. It is often observed that facility managers either are not aware of the new types of sensors (sensor age, set point, and functioning) installed on building systems, or do not examine and calibrate them (Fisk *et al.*, 2010). The proper functioning of sensors such as temperature, humidity, and CO_2 is very important to periodically assess the quality of the indoor air (Fisk *et al.*, 2010). Spaces, such as smoking areas, photocopiers, and printing rooms, should be kept isolated and properly ventilated in order to dilute the air contaminants emitted (Daisey *et al.*, 1994). According to Jaakkola and Miettinen (1995), no interior material should emit any harmful substance such as VOCs. Facility managers can help design and construction professionals identify materials with that have no or low harmful emissions. Above all, a proper supply of outside air should always be maintained in an office environment (Casagrande, 2004; Zimmerman, 2011).

Incorporating FM into Core Business Goals

FM is still seen as a profession dealing mainly with cleaning, caretaking, maintenance, and repairs (Axelsson and Davoust, 2010). However, FM comprises a variety of activities relating to human resource management, property management, and quality management, which are related to an organization's business goals (Ma and Liu, 2010). A business model is defined as "the most fundamental description of how a company or an organization makes money" (Axelsson and Davoust, 2010). Axelsson and Davoust (2010) also cite Dr Alexander Osterwalder, who defined a business model as a description of rationale of how a company or organization "creates, delivers and captures value." Business models and corporate strategies focus more on "core business, customer responsiveness and continual improvement of quality" (Alexander, 2003). Customer satisfaction, employee satisfaction, and productivity and organizational efficiency are core to business strategies (Ma and Liu, 2010). The relationship between FM practices and the productivity of employees of an organization has been underscored (Gensler, 2005; Haynes, 2008; Zimmerman, 2011). The work, the work patterns, and also the functional, physical, and environmental needs of employees are changing at a fast pace (Ware and Grantham, 2003; Andrew *et al.*, 2008). According to Alexander (2003), there is an increased pressure on FM to reduce costs but increase flexibility in managing a facility. Organizations are becoming flatter, autonomous, and decentralized (Alexander, 2003; Ware and Grantham, 2003; Andrew *et al.*, 2008). Businesses are shifting their focus on "customer responsiveness, re-engineered business processes, and creating a service edge" (Alexander, 2003). Alexander (2003) proposed that facilities should provide the needed support to changing business needs by improving adaptability, health and comfort, and the potential for new technologies, and by optimizing resource consumption.

The performance of FM significantly affects organizational performance and helps the organization achieve its business goals. For organizational success and sustainability, it is important to integrate FM into the value chain (Ma and Liu, 2010). Likewise, Alexander (2003), Lundgren and Bjork (2004), and the International Facility Management Association (IFMA, 2009) asserted that FM must be incorporated into the core business model of an organization. Madritsch and Ebinger (2011) described two perspectives that organizations adopt while looking at their real estate holdings. First, the real property is considered "a cost center" that is consuming resources from the core business. Second, real property is considered an asset, which is an investment devoted to fulfill the organization's mission and vision. Facility professionals should shift their focus based on these perspectives, so that they can contribute to the organization's business goals. In the first perspective, facility managers must work toward justifying the real property expenditure, whereas in the second perspective, they must deliver strategic value to the organization. IFMA (2009) discussed strategic facility planning and how facilities (and FM) could support organizations in achieving their mission and vision.

The performance of FM is conventionally judged on the basis of service quality and customer satisfaction (Ma and Liu, 2010). It becomes necessary to gauge the effectiveness of FM to reach an understanding of the current conditions of the facility and to postulate changes in FM practices in order to achieve the desired performance (Amaratunga *et al.*, 2000). Cable and Davis (2004) warn that poor FM could result in inadequate facilities that do not support functioning, excess facilities that do not contribute to the mission of their organization, cost inefficiencies, inadequacy, and unavailability of facilities for future needs. A strong FM approach, on the other hand, provides needed support to the organization's mission, the realization of future facility requirements, cost efficiency, and an ability to anticipate the results of current management decisions. According to Lundgren and Bjork (2004), FM is one of the needed support activities for all business needs.

Summary and Conclusions

FM means different things to different people. Four sectors in which FM is implemented are presented in this chapter: education facilities, public sector buildings, healthcare facilities, and office buildings.

> Each industry and every building type are unique in terms of the challenges they present to their FM personnel.

Responsibilities and charges also depend on factors other than the sector in which the facility operates, such as building size, location, services provided, internal policies, and external forces.

From this chapter, one might get the impression that facility managers have four main challenges for each type of building under consideration. This is not true. Issues like sustainability (energy management, air quality, "green" practices, etc.) and technology (advanced controlling and monitoring of building systems, design and construction capabilities, etc.) may be found all across the range of buildings, even though this chapter did not cover it in one building type or another.

> Additional considerations that facility managers may have to deal with include the aging workforce, aging infrastructure, diminishing budgets, emergency preparedness and management plans, strategic planning, project management, life safety issues, cleaning services, and others. Even though none of these items made the list of the top four challenges in each building type, there is no doubt that these items are importan for the day-to-day smooth, effective, and efficient operation of a facility.

Facility managers tend to say that if everything in a building went without any problems or defects, no one would have even noticed that a facility manager is there. It should always be remembered that FM is the function that exists in order to provide the support that an organization needs to fulfill its business goals and mission. The summary presented in this chapter may be useful in determining the challenges faced both in their own and in other industries, but this list can never be considered as a complete and inclusive range of responsibilities.

References

Abramson, P. (2006). Giving students some space. *School Planning & Management*. May. Available at: http://www.peterli.com/spm/resources/articles/archive.php?article_id=1138 (accessed 18 June 2012).

Advisory, Conciliation and Arbitration Service (ACAS). (2005). Changing patterns of work. Available at: http://www.acas.org.uk/media/pdf/q/4/B09_1.pdf (accessed 20 July 2012).

Alexander, K. (2003). A strategy for facilities management. *Facilities*. 21(11/12), 269–274.

Allen, G. (2001). The private finance initiative (PFI). Research Paper 01/117, 18 December. London: Economic Policy and Statistics Section, House of Commons Library.

Amaratunga, D., Baldry, D., and Sarshar, M. (2000). Assessment of facilities management performance – what next? *Facilities*. 18(1/2), 66–75.

American Federation of Teachers. (2006). *Building minds, minding buildings: turning crumbling schools into environments for learning*. Washington, DC: American Federation of Teachers.

Andrew, J.S., Chang, N., and Nicholson, M. (2008). Office space, changing workplaces and human performance. Kingston, Canada: National Executive Forum on Public Property, Queen's University.

Arge, K. (2005). Adaptable office buildings: theory and practice. *Facilities*. 23(3), 119–127.

American Society for Healthcare Engineering (ASHE). (2004). *Healthcare energy guidebook: results of the Healthcare Energy Project, December 2001 through December 2003*. Chicago, IL: American Society for Healthcare Engineering.

American Society for Testing and Materials (ASTM). (2010). *Standard practice for measuring life-cycle costs of buildings and building systems*. E917-05. West Conshohocken, PA: ASTM.

AutoDesk (2008). BIM and facilities management. AutoDesk white paper. Available at: http://www.microdesk.com/LinkClick.aspx?fileticket=YtBHxydvg-g%3D&tabid=95 (accessed 24 June 2012).

Axelsson, P., and Davoust, T. (2010). *Facilities management – friend or foe?* Lund, Sweden: Industrial Engineering and Management, Division of Production Management, Lund Institute of Technology, Lund University.

Baek, C.H., and Park, S.H. (2012). Changes in renovation policies in the era of sustainability. *Energy and Buildings*. 47(April), 485–496.

Baldwin, E. (2003). The private finance initiative: what opportunities for facilities management? *Journal of Facilities Management*. 2(1), 54–67.

Bartley, J.M. (2000). APIC state-of-the-art report: the role of infection control during construction in health care facilities. *American Journal of Infection Control*. 28(2), 156–169.

Bazjanac, V. (2001). Acquisition of building geometry in the simulation of energy performance. Paper presented at the 2001 Building Simulation Conference, 13–15 August, Rio de Janeiro, Brazil.

Bazjanac, V., and Crawley, D.B. (1997). The implementation of industry foundation classes in simulation tools for the building industry. In: IBPSA (Ed.), *Proceedings of the Fifth International IBPSA Conference, Building Simulation '97, Prague, Czech Republic*.

Beney, D.R. (1999). Equipment planning is an evolving need within health care facility design. *Engineered Systems*. 16(6), 78.

Bennett, D.H., Fisk, W., Apte, M. G., Wu, X., Trout, A., Faulkner, D., and Sullivan, D. (2012). Ventilation, temperature, and HVAC characteristics in small and medium commercial buildings in California. *Indoor Air*. 22, 309–320.

Bennett, J., and Iossa, E. (2006). Building and managing facilities for public services. *Journal of Public Economics*. 90, 2143–2160.

Bodini, A., Giraud, F., Jeanne, P., Jauniaux, L., and Kluft, J-M. (2004). ESA's new approach to facility management. *ESA Bulletin*. 120(November), 57–61.

Boussabaine, H., Sliteen, S., and Catarina, O. (2012). The impact of hospital bed use on healthcare facilities operational costs: the French perspective. *Facilities*. 30(1), 40–55.

Brand, J.L. (1998). Facilities strategies to support corporate change and flexibility. Available at: http://www.haworth.com/en-us/knowledge/workplace-library/Documents/Facilities-Strategies-to-Support-Corporate-Change-and-Flexibility.pdf (accessed 20 July 2012).

Brochner, J. (2008). Construction contractors integrating into facilities management. *Facilities*. 26(1), 6–15.

Bullen, P., and Love, P. (2011). Factors influencing the adaptive re-use of buildings. *Journal of Engineering, Design and Technology*. 9(1), 32–46.

Cable, J.H., and Davis, J.S. (2004). *Key performance indicators for federal facilities portfolios*. Federal Facilities Council Technical Report 147. Washington, DC: National Academies Press.

Casagrande, R.M. (2004). A win-win for IAQ. Maintenance Solutions. Available at: http://www.facilitiesnet.com/iaq/article/A-WinWin-for-IAQ--1831 (accessed 23 July 2012).

Cash, C., and Twiford, T. (2009). Improving student achievement and school facilities in a time of limited funding. Available at: http://cnx.org/content/m23100/latest/ (accessed 12 January 2012).

CBRE (2011). Retrofitting existing buildings: the low cost, high volume solution to climate change. *Sustainability*. 4(Asia Pacific Issue), 11–15.

Chang, H., Kato, S., and Chikamoto, T. (2004). Effects of outdoor air conditions on hybrid air conditioning based on task/ambient strategy with natural and mechanical ventilation in office buildings. *Building and environment*. 39(2), 153–164.

Collins, T.N., and Parson, K.A. (2010). School climate and student outcomes. *Journal of Cross-Disciplinary Perspectives in Education*. 3(1), 34–39.

Crawley, D.B., *et al.* (2005). *Contrasting the capabilities of building energy performance simulation programs*. Washington, DC: US Department of Energy, University of Strathclyde, and University of Wisconsin.

Daisey, J. M., *et al.* (1994). Volatile organic compounds in twelve California office buildings: classes, concentrations and sources. *Atmospheric Environment.* 28(22), 3557–3562.

Douglas, J. (1993–1994). Developments in appraising the total performance of buildings. *Structural Survey.* 12(6), 10–15.

Douglas, J. (1996). Building performance and its relevance to facilities management. *Facilities.* 14(3/4), 23–32.

Duffy, F. (2000). Design and facilities management in a time of change. *Facilities.* 18(10), 371–375.

Earthman, G.I. (2002). *School Facility Conditions and Student Academic Achievement.* Los Angeles: UCLA's Institute for Democracy, Education and Access, University of California.

Eisele-Dyrli, K.R. (2010). School safety gets the ax, districts are struggling to maintain safety when budgets are cut. *District Administration.* 46(8), 52–60.

Erickson, P.W (2010). Tracking costs. *American School & University.* 82, No. 10.

Evans, M.R., and Henderson, D.K. (2005). Infection control in healthcare facilities in the 21st century, business briefing. *Hospital Engineering and Facilities Management.* Available at: http://www.touchbriefings.com/pdf/1618/Henderson.pdf (accessed 19 July 2012).

Fife, G.A. (2006). *2006 middle school prototype, space requirements and special conditions.* Las Vegas, NV: New School and Facility Planning. Clark County School District.

Fisk, W.J, Sullivan, D.P., Faulkner, D., and Eliseeva, E. (2010). *CO2 monitoring for demand controlled ventilation in commercial buildings.* Berkeley, CA: Environmental Energy Technologies Division, Indoor Environment Department, Lawrence Berkeley National Laboratory.

Forster, A.M., and Kayan, B. (2009). Maintenance for historic buildings: a current perspective. *Structural Survey.* 27(3), 210–229.

Fuller, S. K. (2005). *Guidance of life-cycle cost analysis required by Executive Order 13123, April 2005.* Gaithersburg, MD: Building and Fire Research Laboratory, National Institute of Standards and Technology.

Fuller, S. (2010). Life-cycle cost analysis (LCCA). *Whole building design guide.* Available at: http://www.wbdg.org/resources/lcca.php (accessed 14 July 2012).

General Services Administration (GSA) (2011). *BIM Guide for Facility Management.* Washington, DC: General Services Administration.

Gensler. (2005). *These four walls the real British office.* London: Gensler Architecture, Design and Planning Worldwide.

Gomez, A., and Carnero, M.C. (2011). Selection of a computerised maintenance management system: a case study in a regional health service. *Production Planning & Control: The Management of Operations.* 22(4), 426–436.

Haasl, T. (1999). *Operation and maintenance assessments – a best practice for energy-efficient building operations.* Portland, OR: Operation and Maintenance Best Practices, Portland Energy Conservation.

Hammad, A., Fazio, P., and He, H.S. (2005). Computer tool to achieve better performance and integration of building envelopes with structural and mechanical systems. Paper presented at the 33rd Annual General Conference of the Canadian Society for Civil Engineering, 2–4 June, Toronto, ON, Canada.

Hamza, N., and Horne, M. (2007). Building information modeling: empowering energy conscious design. Paper presented at the 3rd International ASCAAD Conference on Embodying Virtual Architecture, 28–30 November, Alexandria, Egypt.

Haynes, B.P. (2008). The impact of office layout on productivity. *Journal of Facilities Management*. 6(3), 189–201.

Heerwagen, J., Kelly, K., and Kampschroer, K. (2005). *Changing nature of organizations, work & workplace*. Washington, DC: General Services Administration.

Heider, E.J., and Brockman, C. (2010). Initial cost and life cycle value of a living hospital building. *FacilityCare*. May–June, 28–31.

International Facility Management Association (IFMA) (2009). *Strategic facility planning: a white paper*. Houston, TX: International Facility Management Association.

Jaakkola, J. J., and Miettinen, P. (1995). Ventilation rate in office buildings and sick building syndrome. *Occupational and Environmental Medicine*. 52(11), 709–714.

JCC (2011). *Computer-aided facilities management (CAFM): fact sheet*. San Francisco: Administrative Office of the Court.

Jones, D.R. (1960). Space: how organized, K-12. *Educational Leadership*. 17(April), 416–464.

Kahn, N. (2009). Healthcare: tides of change. *Health Environments Research & Design Journal*. 3(1), 3–4.

Kats, G. (2006). Greening America's schools, costs and benefits: a Capital E report. Available at: www.cap-e.com (accessed 26 June 2013).

Keller, C. (2005). Effective implementation of automated facility management technology demands culture, process change. *Building Operating Management*, April. Available at: http://www.facilitiesnet.com/BuildingAutomation/article/Automation-One-Step-At-a-Time--2732 (accessed 5 July 2013).

Kirk, S. J. (1996). Life cycle costing for value enhanced healthcare. Paper presented at the SAVE International Conference, May, Chicago, IL.

Krus, C.H. (2004). Analysis of life cycle cost methods for heating, ventilation, and air conditioning systems in hospitals. Master's thesis, University of Texas–Austin.

Lavy, S, Garcia, J.A, and Dixit, M.K. (2010). Establishment of KPIs for facility performance measurement: review of literature. *Facilities*. 28(9), 440–464.

Lavy, S., and Shohet, I.M. (2004). Integrated maintenance management of hospital buildings: a case study. *Construction Management and Economics*. 22(1), 25–34.

London Mallee Region (LMR) (2003). Infection control principles for the management of construction, renovation, repairs and maintenance within health care facilities. Available at: http://www.ihea.org.au/files/Infection ControlManual.pdf (accessed 19 July 2012).

Lundgren, B., and Björk, B. C. (2004). A model integrating the facilities management process with the building end user's business process (ProFacil). *Nordic Journal of Surveying and Real Estate Research*. 1(2), 190–204.

Lyons, J.B. (2001). Do school facilities really impact a child's education? An introduction to the issues. Scottsdale, AZ: Council of Educational Facility Planners International.

Ma, Y., and Liu, K. (2010). Impact analysis of facilities management outsourcing – through a case study of Cisco HQ building. Paper presented at the Intelligent Control and Automation (WCICA) 8th World Congress on IEEE, July.

Madritsch, T., and Ebinger, M. (2011). Performance measurement in facility management the environment management maturity model BEM3. *Research Journal of Economics, Business and ICT*. 2, 4–10.

Madritsch, T., and May, M. (2008). Decision support by computer aided facility management. Paper presented at the CIB W070 Conference on Facility Management, 16–18 June, Heriot Watt University, Edinburgh.

Maile, T., Fischer, M., Bazjanac, V. (2010). A method to compare measured and simulated data to assess building energy performance. Stanford, CA: Center for Integrated Facility Engineering, Civil and Environmental Engineering Department.

McGowen, R.N. (2007). The impact of school facilities on student achievement, attendance, behavior, completion rate and teacher turnover rate in selected Texas high schools. PhD thesis, Texas A&M University, College Station.

Meng, X., and Minogue, M. (2011). Performance measurement models in facility management: a comparative study. *Facilities*. 29(11), 472–484.

Miller, H. (2001). Office alternatives: working on-site. Available at: http://hermanmiller.com/hm/content/research_summaries/wp_Office_Alternatives.pdf (accessed 20 July 2012).

Mitchell, J., Wong, J., and Plume, J. (2007). Design collaboration using IFC: a case study of thermal analysis. In *Computer-aided architectural design futures (CAADFutures)*. Berlin: Springer, pp. 317–329.

Ness, R., and Teicholz, E. (2000). Web-technology: the impact on facility management is just beginning. Available at: http://www.graphicsystems.biz/gsi/articles/Web_Technology_00Sept.pdf (accessed 23 June 2012).

NewSchools Venture Fund (2008). Facilities management and maintenance: key strategies from newschools' portfolio ventures. San Francisco: NewSchools Venture Fund.

Noskin, G.A., and Peterson, L.R. (2001). Engineering infection control through facility design. *Emerging Infectious Diseases*. 7(2), 354.

Nutt, B. (2000). Four competing futures for facility management. *Facilities*. 18(3), 124–132.

O'Neill, M. (2008). *A model of environmental control and effective work*. East Greenville, PA: Knoll Workplace Research.

Palmer, E. (2012). *3 game-changing trends of the modern office*. Wrike, Practical Project Management. Available at: http://www.wrike.com/blog/01/31/2012/3-Game-Changing-Trends-Modern-Office (accessed 20 July 2012).

Patterson, M. (2008). Design from a facilities management perspective. *Medical Construction & Design*. July/August, 46–48.

Rich, S., and Davis, K.H. (2010). *Geographic information systems (GIS) for facility management*. Houston, TX: IFMA Foundation.

RIDE. (2007). *RIDE school construction regulations*. Providence, RI: Rhode Island Department of Education.

Riley, D., Freihaut, J., Bahnfleth, W.P., and Karapatyan, Z. (2006). Indoor air quality management and infection control in health care facility construction. IAQ T3S1 Innovative Techniques in IAQ. Available at: http://www.engr.psu.edu/iec/publications/papers/indoor_air_quality.pdf (accessed 5 July 2013).

Sadler, B.L., Berry, L.L., and Guenther, R. (2011). Fable hospital 2.0: the business case for building better health care facilities. *The Hastings Center Report*. 41(1), 13–22.

Saporta, R., Ellis, R., and Kwok, M. (2008). O&M cost management for health-care facility. *ASHRAE Journal*. March, 34–41.

Sapp, D. (2011). Computerized maintenance management systems (CMMS): whole building design guide. Available at: http://www.wbdg.org/om/cmms.php (accessed 24 June 2012).

Schneider, M. (2002). *Do school facilities affect academic outcomes?* Washington, DC: National Clearinghouse for Educational Facilities.

Schneider Electric. (2006). *Leading techniques for energy savings in healthcare facilities*. North Andover, MA: Schneider Electric.

Schroeder, C.G., Baird, J., Roberts, K.B., and Cohen, G.L. (1995). Studies for the development of a space utilization index. USACERL Technical Report 95/34, September. Washington, DC: US Army Corps of Engineers.

Seppanen, O., Fisk, W.J., and Lei, Q.H. (2006). Ventilation and performance in office work. *Indoor Air*. 16(1), 28–36.

Singer, B.C., and Tschudi, W.F. (2009). *High performance healthcare buildings: a roadmap to improved energy efficiency*. Report No. LBNL-2737E. Berkeley, CA: Ernest Orlando Lawrence Berkeley National Laboratory.

Stichler, J.F. (2010). Nurses' caps, ballgames, and hard hats. *Health Environments Research & Design Journal*. 3(2), 7–12.

Sullivan, G.P., Pugh, R., Melendez, A. P., and Hunt, W. D. (2010). *Operations and maintenance best practices: a guide to achieving operational efficiency*. Release 3.0. Washington, DC: Federal Energy Management Program, US Department of Energy.

Tanis, J., and Duffy, F. (1999). A vision of the new workplace revisited. *Site Selection Magazine*. September, 805–814.

Ticer, J. (2011). Integrating medical equipment planning into the construction process. *Health Facilities Management*. 24(5).

Trump, K.S. (2004). Trends in school and emergency preparedness, planning: keeping school administrators "in the know" and out of the spotlight. *School Planning & Management and Today's School*. Suppl., 16–20.

Trump, K.S. (2009). School emergency planning: back to the basics, "nuts-and-bolts" details make or break schools in a crisis. *Student Assistance Journal*. Spring, 12–17.

Tsai, D.H., Lin, J.S., and Chan, C.C. (2012). Office worker's sick building syndrome and indoor carbon dioxide concentrations. *Journal of Occupational and Environmental Hygiene*. 9(5), 345–351.

US Department of Energy (USDOE) (2010a). *Guide to operating and maintaining energy smart schools*. Washington, DC: US Department of Energy.

US Department of Energy (USDOE) (2010b). *Guide to financing energy smart schools*. Washington, DC: US Department of Energy.

US Department of Energy (USDOE) (2010c). *Annual energy review 2010*. Washington, DC: Energy Information Administration, US Department of Energy.

US Environmental Protection Agency (EPA) (1991). *Building air quality: a guide for building owners and facility managers*. Washington, DC: EPA.

US Environmental Protection Agency (EPA) (2011). *Energy efficiency programs in K–12 schools: a guide to developing and implementing greenhouse gas reduction programs*. Washington, DC: US Department of Energy.

Vittori, G. (2011). Greening of healthcare: locations and design of facilities are essential to the mission of health. *Modern Healthcare*. Anniversary issue, 42.

Wang, H.J, Chiou, C., and Juan, Y. (2008). Decision support model based on case-based reasoning approach for estimating the restoration budget of historical buildings. *Expert Systems with Applications*. 35(4), 1601–1610.

Ware, H., and Grantham, C. (2003). The future of work: changing patterns of workforce management and their impact on the workplace. *Journal of Facilities Management*. 2(2), 142–159.

Wargocki, P., *et al*. (2000). The effects of outdoor air supply rate in an office on perceived air quality, sick building syndrome (SBS) symptoms and productivity. *Indoor Air*. 10(4), 222–236.

Watson, B.M., Strong, C., and Bunting B. (2008). *Severe weather planning for schools*. Washington, DC: National Clearinghouse for Educational Facilities at the National Institute of Building Sciences.

Young, E., *et al*. (2003). *Do K–12 school facilities affect education outcomes?* Nashville, TN: Tennessee Advisory Commission on Intergovernmental Relations.

Zimmerman, G. (2011). Facility occupants can breathe easier when facility managers have good data. *Building Operating Management*. Available at: http://www.facilitiesnet.com/iaq/article/Facility-Occupants-Can-Breathe-Easier-When-Facility-Managers-Have-Good-Data--12526# (accessed 23 July 2012).

Zimring, C. (2010). Facility performance evaluation (FPE): whole building design guide. Available at: http://www.wbdg.org/resources/fpe.php (accessed 12 July 2012).

Evolution and the Future of Facility Management

Kathy O. Roper

Georgia Institute of Technology, Atlanta, GA

"And it ought to be remembered that there is nothing more difficult to handle, more doubtful of success, and more dangerous to carry through than initiating change." Machiavelli recognized in the early 1500s that human nature resisted change, but little in over 500 years has evolved regarding humans' opposition to change (Machiavelli, 1995). However, we know that with technology, science, and new patterns of work and social life, change is occurring more rapidly and with more impact than ever before. This is also true in the management of the built environment, with miniaturization, advanced integration of software, and information and communication technologies (ICT) becoming more capable of supporting anywhere, anytime work. The workforces that we support, as well as our own facility management (FM) staff, have new tools, new ways of working, and new analytical capabilities requiring change and adaptation.

This chapter provides an overview of how FM as a profession was developed and its rapid evolution. The primary driver of workplace change is and has been technology. Advancements quickly improve workers' ability to gather and process information in an anywhere, anytime environment. Technology is also changing buildings and how they are designed, constructed, and operated.

Evolution of FM

When the term *facility management* was adopted in the 1970s, the workplace was in flux. The need for someone to understand, plan for, and manage the new office environment created the change that allowed

International Facility Management, First Edition. Kathy O. Roper and Lisa J. Borello.
© 2014 John Wiley & Sons, Ltd. Published 2014 by John Wiley & Sons, Ltd.

FM as a profession to develop. And development has been continuous since that time. The facility manager moved from being an order taker to advising the organization on space and workplace issues. Reduction in operating costs was a central focus for much of the late twentieth century, while in the early twenty-first century, the profession has evolved into recognizing, demonstrating, and adding value. The facility manager has become a true business manager, aiding strategic decision making with financial, market, and built-environment expertise. The tools in FM have evolved from hard-copy drawings and pen-and-paper order forms to computer-aided facility management (CAFM) and integrated workplace management systems (IWMS), and now building information modeling (BIM) is becoming integrated throughout the life cycle of buildings, providing further integration of technologies.

Technology has enabled a somewhat reduced workforce; many organizations have partnered with third-party providers for facility services expertise, and today the facility professional is expected to possess an extremely broad range of knowledge from maintenance and operations to real estate, leadership, and communications skills, as well as finance, technology, and project expertise. Facility managers must know something about all areas of the organization they support to enable strategic planning, as well as know about new technologies and integrated facility services contracting, local building codes and regulations, sustainability measures, and certification standards. The effective leader of a facility organization is also a strong personnel manager, organizing the best mix of contracts, staff, and one-off project management in order to allow the organization's workforce to operate at maximum productivity and least cost.

Today, FM functions are often allocated in large companies across a divergent group of organizations. Many of the risk, regulatory compliance, and related functions are moved to Legal or Risk Management departments. As the facility professional remains responsible for safety and compliance with regulations regarding the workplace and the built environment, the facility manager must maintain strong relationships with the Legal and Risk departments within the company. As more functions are outsourced to specialty or integrated service providers, the FM becomes more aware and skilled in negotiation, and often relies on the Procurement or Purchasing departments for their assistance in executing best value contracts for these resources. With sustainability at the forefront of change within most organizations, the FM is required to understand, recommend, and justify sustainability measures for the organization's workplace, bringing new skill sets and knowledge requirements. These specializations across multiple departments within a company require excellent communication and that shared information among these departments is available to everyone involved. Technologies have helped make shared databases and access to information easier; however, the challenge is to always ensure that the data are updated and accurate. This is one of the shifts in skills and services that facility organizations must provide to ensure that their recommendations and decision-making processes accurately reflect the current and future state.

As personnel in FM transition from individual experience as their primary source of data to reliance on electronic databases of information, technology skills take precedence. This is one indicator of the change that directly impacts facility organizations – relying on accurate data for decision making.

In some cases, integration of systems may free humans from some decisions that can be programmed, such as building automation systems (BAS) that monitor indoor environment conditions and self-adjust to provide consistent conditions as preprogrammed by the facility professionals. This then frees humans to address more strategic issues than checking thermostats and adjusting temperature and humidity controls, and it makes the facility organization more valuable through the appropriate use of technology.

Technologies and Future FM

Just as society has evolved from dramatically different work styles when moving from the Agrarian Age into the Industrial Age, mature societies have now moved beyond the Industrial Age into the Knowledge Age and are still managing the transition from old, industrial, machine-age management thought into evolved performance metrics that consider collaborative, creative skills essential for the workforce of today and tomorrow. Mechanical power has fallen in favor of "brain power" and knowledge work. Successful FM professionals and FM departments are also making major changes to support knowledge work and adapt technology, societal change, and ICT mobility as tools to improve the workplace and the organizations they support.

General and Building Technologies

One of the most obvious changes to facility professionals is the advancement of technologies that support the operation of the built environment. Automation of systems and the integration of information across multiple platforms allow for more rapid and independent control of the building environment. Today's workplaces have become a complex network of diverse needs. Whether it is precise control of temperature and humidity for worker comfort or process control or monitoring of critical components, such as lighting, fuel tanks, and power systems, advanced technologies allow a more accurate and controllable building. Additional integrations may involve providing secure authorized access control for time and attendance or for security access, alarm monitoring, and fire and smoke detection. All of the systems maintained by an FM group can be automated and integrated to some degree. And as facility managers demand more integration, the marketplace is responding, allowing fewer independent systems and easier integration across system platforms.

In the near future, the continuing advancement of integration may enable a "one-stop shop" for FM automation. Full integration of enterprise information integration will speed the ability of organizations to immediately disable security access at an employee termination, or track enterprise accounting of charges from the receipt of a service request through completion and even into budget allocation and input for next-year financial planning. Once the details are programmed, each transaction component is automated to feed into other integrated systems, saving countless labor hours from FM staff.

Future possibilities include increased miniaturization of sensors; for example, paints will be embedded with sensors to register temperature, humidity, or other conditions that can feed wirelessly into the BAS and improve the operation and aesthetics of the office. Other technologies are embedding computer and projection screens into building surfaces, like walls and panels, so that these screens pop up from the building surfaces themselves as needed, and these may also become three-dimensional (3D) or even holographic, providing more life-like interaction possibilities.

Security enhancements are also becoming embedded into the structure of buildings, such as epoxy additives to building waterproofing coatings that also have blast ratings. Sensors that are able to track or alarm whenever someone enters a space can be embedded into the coatings and can provide unseen security measures where needed.

Other innovative buildings are being designed to "clean" the air as it is filtered through portions of the structure, providing the surrounding area with less polluted air. Net-zero buildings that contain enough self-supporting power generation to provide all the power needed within the building are being designed and constructed for future needs that require dramatically reduced utility provision.

Additional technologies are being researched today that will make our buildings more self-supporting, more secure, more flexible for anticipated changes, and also more user compatible and welcoming – these technologies will all enhance and change the nature of the facility management profession.

FM Software

Along with emerging technologies, new software to help manage facilities is rapidly expanding and, in many cases, becoming more integrated. Historically, software has been developed to meet specific needs, and many times the software development process does not include research to learn what portions of information may already be available or may not easily translate into the software, requiring duplicate work to enter data into a second system. This issue is at the heart of software integrations that are occurring across the built-environment field. Facility professionals often manage multiple functions, each with its own dedicated software. Computerized maintenance management systems are for maintenance and operations functions, and computer-aided facility management (CAFM) and IWMS are for space planning, move and space management, along with accounting additions to charge users for space, commonly referred to as chargebacks. BAS provide sensing and automation to help control heating, ventilation, and air conditioning (HVAC) primarily. Additional fire safety systems, security access control systems, and perhaps uninterrupted power systems (UPS) with battery back-up are also managed. These may not relate to or integrate with real estate systems to manage leases, administer master planning for owned spaces, or tie into any related departmental systems such as human resource databases, IT equipment inventories, or other operational systems within the company.

Ideally, technology integration would provide one-time entry of information, such as employee data, space and infrastructure systems data, or related details from facility management and other departments. As more standardization is occurring globally, these goals for integration are becoming reality. BIM offers a solution to many built-environment integration issues since, theoretically, layers of information in BIM could be unlimited (at a cost, of course). More discussion of BIM integration follows in the "Project Management Developments" section, but even BIM is not the ultimate solution. Facility management professionals need to advocate for their own needs in order to bring such solutions into the marketplace. To truly increase value to an organization's FM support, improved software integration is a crucial step.

Project Management Developments

One of the most dramatic changes in recent years has been the acceptance of the synergistic impacts of sustainability, integrated project delivery (IPD), and BIM. These three areas have been shown to produce dramatic improvements, especially when used in combination. Various examples of construction projects focused on one of these components resulted in a better building, but project team members have noted that when all three efforts are combined, the projects are much better planned and, therefore, result in an improved product with less delay, more collaboration, and often less cost.

From the Building Research Establishment Environmental Assessment Method (BREEAM) in the United Kingdom, to Leadership in Energy and Environmental Design (LEED) in the United States, and to Green Globes and many other sustainability guidelines for the built environment across the world, more companies are deciding to build more sustainably. This applies not only to the initial design and construction, but also thankfully to the huge operational phase of the building life cycle, the occupancy and operation of the building. Since this is often 80–90% of the full life-cycle cost of the building, the focus on this phase is receiving more and more attention. As FM professionals have long recognized the need for investment to maintain and operate the building at maximum efficiency, the sustainability focus has given the broader population knowledge about the full life-cycle cost of a building. Of course, investors want to save money in the initial cost of constructing a building, but no longer is the operational cost ignored by insightful organizations, which require full life-cycle costing before making final building design decisions. Bringing facility management professionals into the discussion very early on in the development process results in a more flexible, efficient, and sustainable building. The issues of usability, operability, and maintainability are discussed and resolved in the initial process, avoiding later, costly changes once the building is occupied.

Relatedly, the use of a new methodology for integrating all project stakeholders very early in the development process has been successfully launched. Integrated project delivery (IPD) is the term used for these projects that bring the constructor, the users, and the facility operators into the development and design discussion. Currently, there is not a fully developed definition that has been vetted in the FM community, but the American Institute of Architects and Associated General Contractors of America (2011) defined IPD as a delivery method based on the idea of collaboration:

> IPD is a method of project delivery distinguished by a contractual arrangement among a minimum of the owner, constructor and design professional that aligns business interests of all parties. IPD motivates collaboration throughout the design and construction process, tying stakeholder success to project success, and embodies the following contractual and behavioral principles:
>
> Contractual Principles – Key Participants Bound Together as Equals; Shared Financial Risk and Reward Based on Project Outcome; Liability Waivers between Key Participants; Fiscal Transparency between Key Participants; Early Involvement of Key Participants; Jointly Developed Project Target Criteria; and Collaborative Decision Making.

Behavioral Principles – Mutual Respect and Trust; Willingness to Collaborate; and Open Communication.

While this definition continues to evolve, the focus of bringing all stakeholders into early discussions on the project has proven beneficial from a cost, timeline, and satisfaction standpoint – the three key deliverables of any project.

BIM is the use of digital representation of both physical and functional aspects of a building. For facility management, the "information" is the primary focus, although digital models can also be helpful to clients for visualizing future designs, providing construction prefabrication applications, and providing clash detection of building components prior to finalization of design and construction specification. The information provided during design and construction is entered into the BIM database and therefore available immediately after occupancy for operational enhancements. However, this information input is not guaranteed, nor is it even provided in many cases today. The facility professional must promote and even demand that this information be captured in the design and construction phases, in order to benefit from the data once operations begin.

Detailed information on building components, systems, furniture, and even finishes are becoming easier to input into BIM databases due to Industry Foundation Class (IFC) standardization and product manufacturer acceptance of IFC classifications. Ideally, when the design is finalized, IFC data are pulled from the manufacturer's specifications and downloaded into BIM. Later, during use of the building, the IFC information is available to the facility manager when maintenance, repair, or replacement is required.

People Aspects of Future FM

Along with technology, the softer human skills are also changes that are occurring within the profession and will continue to change as FM evolves. Based on the mechanical and technical competencies to operate a building, initially FM professionals focused on enhancing these skills.

Today, technological skills are still required, but with automation, integration, and outsourcing, facility professionals have advanced to take on business, financial, and communication skills, increasing the value they bring to the supported organization.

A number of leadership skills, often referred to as "soft skills," are needed for facility managers of the future:

- Change management
- Charisma

- Client relationship management
- Communication
- Creativity
- Critical thinking
- Culture of learning

These seven skills can be cultivated in facility professionals and are encouraged for leading facility organizations into the future. While some may seem innate, such as "charisma," the focus is really on being able to recognize and utilize techniques to influence others to obtain needed results. Senior executive courses offer instruction in many of these soft skills and are required to negotiate the complex environment found in organizations today, and specific tools and techniques can enhance success in all of these areas. First, awareness that the skills are needed and beneficial is a major change from historic facility management training and experience. Next is the training and improvement needed for facility professionals to become proficient in all of these skills; without them, limitations will be found in dynamic organizational processes.

As organizations continue to change, the workplace arrangements and support that FM departments provide continues to change. As technology advances, we are required to work with our clients to update or adapt to new technologies. Change management techniques, an entire field of research and process, can be used to successfully transition users to new forms, new service-level agreements, and new ways of working in and out of the office. Societies for change management exist, similar to those that support FM. The Association of Change Management Professionals is one good resource for additional information (www.acmpglobal.org).

Charisma is considered by some to be an innate trait that one either does or does not possess. But even those not possessing innate charisma can learn techniques to help increase their influence and persuasive ability. Research on brain activity and processes provides some guides, and those that are developed by Robert Cialdini to use positivity, sharing of information, and good deeds can accelerate one's persuasive ability over command-and-control types of leadership domination (Cialdini, 2006).

Client relationship management (CRM) is a tool that originated in the customer service organization field to more fully understand and anticipate clients' needs and expectations. Internal CRM for facility management to focus on users is an important tool that requires resources to focus on individual business units to fully understand their motivations, needs, and strategic plans. Rather than simply asking what your facility needs are, the CRM aspect of FM delves into the business drivers for each department to more fully understand what drives that specific portion of the business. The better a facility professional understands the client, the better prepared to anticipate and provide those needed services or spaces the FM department will be. This moves FM from reactionary to proactive delivery of user needs. Fully understanding client needs also allows for better decision making when various reconfigurations, reallocations, or changes are needed in workplaces.

The importance of communication cannot be overstated for any facility professional. Not only providing information but also listening actively and proactively demonstrating understanding of users' needs are critical. Since FM deals with all levels of the organization, from CEO to entry-level employees and from vendors to long-time staff, various communication delivery models and methods should be used for most facility information. Users may need multiple versions of a communication to finally understand its intent. Some users need visual information, others prefer more text-oriented delivery, while some may even prefer auditory information, delivered via voicemail or video delivery. Always considering multiple audiences and multiple delivery methods can improve communication of facility information. A basic communication skill is active listening – this is a skill that can be practiced with beneficial effects.

Creativity may be a skill that has been put aside by facility professionals as they conform to standards and policies. But creativity and innovation have become valuable skills that all employees and especially facility employees should resurrect. Innovative companies have been using relaxing and entertaining environments for years to stimulate and refocus their employees' brain power. These techniques can also be adapted to FM without providing basketball courts or indoor slides and pool tables. The simple use of fun and games in the workplace can often stimulate teamwork and new thoughts. The use of true brainstorming, avoiding judgment in the initial development of ideas, is a wonderful tool to create new ideas and creative solutions to issues. Too often, the brainstorming process is cut short with comments such as "That will not work" or "That costs too much," but the key is to throw out wild and crazy ideas without judgment, which may spark other more realistic ideas during the process. Later, in the prioritization stages of brainstorming, the unrealistic ideas can be eliminated, but in the initial stages, the crazier the better. Other techniques for introducing and encouraging creativity can be found with any Google search of "creativity."

Critical thinking is a higher level skill that is important to bring to the management of the built environment. Too often, speed in decision making results in errors and costly mistakes. A few critical thinking skills, like questioning the source of information or searching for biases in decision making, can improve critical thinking and, therefore, decision making. Especially in today's environment of free information sources, not all are reliable, and sources should always be questioned for authority and knowledge. Just because a vendor's website states that a 30% improvement can be gained does not guarantee that your benchmarked costs will be improved. Learning the background of an employee's education and prior experience may help to avoid overly biased preferences. Establishing the initial premise of an issue or documenting the full design intent for a new building could be examples of information that will aid future decision making with more critical thinking.

A culture of learning is a newer trend in business today that encourages new ideas and expanded thinking and provides the resources to back up this culture. Training on new techniques, tools, and skills, and even dedicated time to learn new equipment, software, and other tools, are mandatory to remain at the top of all employees' skill levels. Without this culture and motivation for learning, with rapid advancements in business, future skills may not be met.

One new facet of FM is the new formal education programs around the world offering degrees in FM. The International Facility Management Association (IFMA) Foundation has a formal accreditation process for schools teaching FM and has accredited more than 20 schools' programs at various degree levels. As universities learn of the growing demand for FM education, new programs are launching in emerging economies, and areas of the world are developing these programs to meet the rapid demand. In a recent discussion with Indian development professionals (B. Agarwal, Managing Director, Sattva Group, personal communication, February 10, 2012) who anticipate approximately 500 new airport facilities to be built across India within the next 10 years, they recognize that individuals need education and training to manage, operate, and maintain these new facilities. Discussions across India about new facility training and education programs mean that many more degreed facility managers will be available in the next decade. Other areas of the world are also expanding their knowledge and interest in FM, and the future for the profession is bright.

Related to the soft skills is the need to become networked and partner with internal and external partners. Primary relationships with the internal departments managing information technology (IT) and human resources (HR), as well as purchasing and accounting, are necessary. Any facility project will require interaction with, and possibly dependence on, any or all of these other internal departments. Without following company purchasing policies and without the purchasing department's assistance, the contracts and procurement processes needed on a day-to-day basis in FM could be compromised. A minor relocation project could be jeopardized if the IT department is not in alignment with client and FM needs and the schedule for the project.

In their book *Workplace Flexibility*, Christensen and Schneider (2010) comment on numerous global initiatives to allow workers more flexibility in worker productivity. The benefits and drivers of these programs are diverse, but the key finding is that regardless of whether the impetus for change included reducing energy, as in one Australian program, or providing work–life balance in Japan, the organization as well as the individual workers benefitted from the changes. This type of evidence – that benefits can be gained on both employer and employee sides of the issue – needs better dissemination and discussion in business journals and schools.

Summary and Conclusions

The world is changing, business is changing, and FM must change to keep pace and continue to provide value. With developing formal education programs in FM, new research on methodologies and skills, and added focus on the value from the total life-cycle costs of buildings in the forefront of discussions across the world, the future for FM is rapidly expanding and is becoming more recognized and valued, and it is an important profession. Change is inevitable, and FM is changing to improve just as rapidly as business, technology, and the societies it supports.

The ongoing advancement in technologies will continue to impact our facilities and the workers utilizing them. Robotics, nanotechnology, augmented and virtual realities, and a host of new technologies will impact the management of the built environment in ways that we cannot even imagine today. Embracing change and working to stay current on changes are required for effective facility management, and we can continue to expect continuing change. To sum it up, as baseball's Yogi Berra is quoted as saying, "The future ain't what it used to be."

References

American Institute of Architects and Associated General Contractors of America. (2011). *Primer on project delivery*. 2nd ed. Washington, DC: American Institute of Architects and Associated General Contractors of America.

Christensen, K., and Schneider, B. (Eds.). (2010). *Workplace flexibility*. Ithaca, NY: Cornell University Press.

Cialdini, R. (2006). *Influence: the psychology of persuasion*. New York: William Morrow.

Machiavelli, N. (1995). *The prince*. Translated and Edited by Stephen J. Milner. New York: Everyman.

Index

Note: Page numbers in *italics* refer to Figures; those in **bold** to Tables.

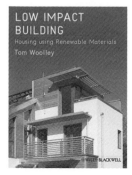
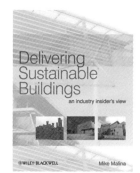
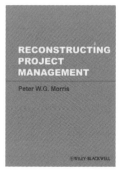